MAN OF VALOR

*Every Man's Quest
for a Life of
Honor, Conviction, and Character*

RICHARD EXLEY

WHITE STONE BOOKS
LAKELAND, FLORIDA

Published in association with Yates & Yates, LLP, Attorneys and Counselors, Orange, California

10 09 08 07 06 05   10 9 8 7 6 5 4 3 2 1

Man of Valor:
Every Man's Quest for a Life of Honor, Conviction, and Character

ISBN 1–59379–027–9
Copyright © 2005 by Richard Exley
P. O. Box 54744
Tulsa, Oklahoma 74155

Published by White Stone Books, Inc.
P.O. Box 2835
Lakeland, Florida 33806

DEDICATION

To the Reverend S. Worth Williams
who was truly a pastor to me.

And

To the Reverend Allen "Tex" Groff
who believed in me when I couldn't believe
in myself and who believes in me still.

✛

CONTENTS

INTRODUCTION

On March 25, 2003, while advancing up Highway 1 toward Baghdad as part of Operation Iraqi Freedom, platoon leader Brian Chontosh and his men were ambushed. Enemy forces bombarded them with mortars, rocket-propelled grenades, and automatic weapons fire. With coalition tanks blocking the road ahead, the marines were trapped in a kill zone.

With no apparent way out, Chontosh ordered the driver of his Humvee to charge the Iraqi machine gun emplacement that was firing at them, enabling his .50 caliber machine gunner to open fire. Within a matter of minutes the enemy machine gun was silenced, the Iraqi soldiers dead or routed.

Chontosh then ordered his driver to take the Humvee directly into the Iraqi trench that housed the enemy soldiers who were attacking his marines. Into the battlement the Humvee went and out the door Brian Chontosh bailed, carrying an M16 and a Beretta and 228 years of Marine Corps pride.

He fought with the M16 until he ran out of ammo. Then he emptied the Beretta. Jamming it into his belt, he picked up a dead Iraqi's AK47 and fought on. When it was out of ammo, he threw it aside and picked up a second AK47, and with total disregard for his personal safety, he continued his ferocious attack. When a marine following him found an enemy rocket-propelled grenade launcher, Chontosh used it to destroy yet another group of enemy soldiers.

When his audacious attack ended, he had cleared over 200 meters of the enemy trench, killing more than 20 enemy soldiers and wounding several others, completely destroying the attempted ambush.[1]

On May 6 , 2004, he was awarded the Navy Cross "for extraordinary heroism while serving as Combined Anti-Armor Platoon Commander, Weapons Company, 3rd Battalion, 5th Marine Regiment, 1st Marine Division, 1st Marine Expeditionary Force, in support of Operation Iraqi Freedom March 25, 2003."

Now that's what comes to mind when I think of a man of valor—courage under fire, heroic action in the face of great danger, and duty above self. It's what most men dream of—a chance to prove that they have what it takes.

Since most of us will never have to participate in combat, we will have to prove our valor in more mundane ways. The enemies attacking us will not be soldiers on a battlefield but the inner enemies that war against our souls— things like fear, egotism, selfishness, materialism, lust, and the abuse of power. These are the enemies that ambush us at every turn, that threaten to rob us of our destiny. And these are the enemies we must defeat if we are to become the men God has called us to be.

In pursuit of this quest, I have identified seven characteristics possessed by valiant men throughout history and today. They are: 1) Spiritual passion; 2) Courage; 3) Loyalty; 4) Integrity; 5) Sexual purity; 6) Wisdom; and 7) Compassion. Using scriptural principles and real life examples I will show you how to cultivate these traits in your lives and become true men of valor.

You may feel it is too late, that you've been robbed of your destiny. Don't give up! God has a plan for your life even if you can't see it. As a man created in His image, you are destined for greatness. Whether you realize it or not you were created to be a valiant man! No matter how foreign that may seem to you, it's true. You were created to conquer! That's what the Bible says, "...Be fruitful, and multiply, and replenish the earth, and subdue it...."[2]

Don't measure your future by your past. God is about to intervene in your life and do a new thing. Let Gideon be your example. He was an ordinary man at best, yet the Lord called him a "...mighty man of valor!"[3] "Then the LORD turned to him and said, 'Go in this might of yours, and you shall save Israel from the hand of the Midianites. Have I not sent you?'"[4]

"...O my Lord," Gideon said, "how can I save Israel? Indeed my clan is the weakest in Manasseh, and I am the least in my father's house."[5]

Does that kind of negative self-talk sound familiar? Have all your efforts to prove your masculinity, whatever form they may have taken—athletic exploits, financial success, sexual escapades, or even feats of courage—all proven futile? Are you convinced that if others knew you as you know yourself, they would see you for the phony you often feel you are? Gideon felt that way too. Yet when the Lord finished with him he was a mighty warrior, a true man of valor who delivered Israel.

Your inner enemies can never be defeated with the carnal weapons of physical prowess or business acumen.

For we are not fighting "...flesh and blood, but against the rulers, against the authorities, against the powers of this dark world and against the spiritual forces of evil in the heavenly realms."[6]

"For though we live in the world, we do not wage war as the world does. The weapons we fight with are not the weapons of the world. On the contrary, they have divine power to demolish strongholds. We demolish arguments and every pretension that sets itself up against the knowledge of God, and we take captive every thought to make it obedient to Christ."[7] The truth—God's truth—is the only weapon that will defeat these enemies and set us free to fulfill our destiny.

Set in devotional format, the following chapters are short and hard-hitting—straight to the point. Utilizing action steps that are designed to help you integrate these principles into your own daily walk, they build one upon the other, day by day, until the false pretenses of the enemy have been replaced by the truth of God.

But enough of that.... Let's get started. Your destiny is calling.

---

[1] Based on Story by Cpl. Jeremy Vought, MCB Camp Pendleton, Story Identification #: 200456162723.
[2] Genesis 1:28 (KJV).
[3] Judges 6:12 (NKJV).
[4] Judges 6:14 (NKJV).
[5] Judges 6:15 (NKJV).
[6] Ephesians 6:12.
[7] 2 Corinthians 10:3-5.

THE FIRST CHARACTERISTIC OF A MAN OF VALOR IS

SPIRITUAL PASSION

*Nothing is more important than
what a man believes about God.
How he perceives Him will determine, to a significant degree,
what he believes about himself and how he relates to others.
It will also define his interpretation
of life and the meaning of events.
Never is a man's understanding of God more
critical than in times of personal crisis.*

CHAPTER 1

THE TRUTH ABOUT GOD

 Are you afraid of God?

Probably not, unless you were raised in a legalistic church as I was. The God of my adolescence was a cross between a medieval executioner and a hanging judge. To me, He was a God Who meted out judgment with sadistic delight and extended forgiveness grudgingly, and then only to the most penitent. The mere thought of Him caused me to tremble in terror. In truth, I feared Him, but I did not love Him.

As a young adult, I rejected the sadistic God of my adolescence. I simply could not live with the kind of fear and condemnation He generated in me. In place of the cruel, unloving God of my youth, I created a kinder and gentler God. Here was a God I could love but I did not revere Him.

Who is the real God—the stern and distant deity of my adolescent years, or the benevolent and kindly father figure with which I replaced Him? Neither? Both? To find the answer we must turn, not to our subjective experiences, but to the eternal Scriptures.

God, as He reveals Himself in Scripture, is altogether holy,[1] absolutely just,[2] and totally righteous.[3] Because He is holy, He cannot tolerate sin. Being just, He cannot allow a single sinful act to go unpunished. And because He is righteous, He cannot fellowship with anyone who does not measure up to His holy standard. In addition, the Scriptures reveal that He is infinite, eternal, and wholly unapproachable. No wonder the ancient Hebrews pleaded with Moses, "...'Speak to us yourself and we will listen. But do not have God speak to us or we will die.'"[4]

Yet, the Scriptures also declare that He is a God of love,[5] mercy,[6] and grace.[7] Being a God of love, He cannot turn His back on fallen humanity without denying that part of His eternal character. And because He is a God of mercy and grace, He cannot allow mankind to be eternally lost without providing for our salvation.

Herein lies the dilemma—how can God be both just and merciful? How can He forgive our sins without betraying His justice? Yet, by the same token, if He does not forgive our sins, will He not betray His love and mercy?

Only the infinite wisdom of God could find a solution, and only the unconditional love of God could make that solution a living reality. Through the incarnation of His Son Jesus, the love and wisdom of God manifest themselves in glorious detail.

By becoming one of us and living a sinless life, Jesus fully satisfied the holy demands of a righteous God,[8] thus making it possible for God to accept us.

Through His sacrificial death, Jesus suffered the full penalty for our sins, thus satisfying the just demands of a holy God, and making it possible for God to forgive our sins without violating His character. Since both His just and righteous demands have been satisfied, God is now free to manifest His love and mercy toward us.

So great is the love of God that there are times when I am tempted to make light of sin, to foolishly think that it is no big thing. Then I remember the Cross! That's what God thinks about sin. It is so deadly, so evil, that it must be dealt with even if it means punishing His own Son. The prophet Isaiah says that Jesus was, "...stricken by God, smitten by him, and afflicted....it was the LORD's will to crush him and cause him to suffer....For he bore the sin of many...."[9] And if ever I am tempted to doubt the absolute love of God, to think that my repeated failures have driven me beyond the reach of His love, I remember the Cross! That's God's love message to me! With iron spikes, broken flesh, and spilled blood, He poured out His love for me—"But God demonstrates his own love for us in this: While we were still sinners, Christ died for us."[10]

And that's the truth about God!

ACTION STEPS:

▼ EXAMINE YOUR IMAGE OF GOD, YOUR UNDERSTANDING OF HIS CHAR-
ACTER AND NATURE. MAKE A LIST OF HIS ATTRIBUTES.

▼ NOW EXAMINE YOUR LIST. ARE THE ATTRIBUTES YOU LISTED BASED ON
SCRIPTURE OR ARE THEY A KIND OF COMPOSITE SKETCH BASED ON
YOUR OWN SUBJECTIVE EXPERIENCES?

▼ CONSCIOUSLY ASK GOD TO REVEAL HIMSELF TO YOU SO THAT YOU
MAY LOVE AND REVERE HIM AS YOU SHOULD.

THOUGHT FOR THE DAY:

"Heavenly Father: Let me see your glory, if it must be from the
shelter of the cleft rock and from beneath the protection of your covering
hand, whatever the cost to me in loss of friends or goods or length of
days let me know you as you are, that I may adore you as I should.
Through Jesus Christ our Lord. Amen."[11]

A .W. Tozer

SCRIPTURE FOR THE DAY:

"Who among the gods is like you, O LORD?
Who is like you—majestic in holiness, awesome in glory, working wonders?
"In your unfailing love you will lead the people you have redeemed.
In your strength you will guide them to your holy dwelling."

EXODUS 15:11,13

PRAYER:

LORD, DELIVER ME FROM MY MISCONCEPTIONS.

LET ME KNOW YOU AS YOU TRULY ARE THAT I MAY WORSHIP

YOU AS I SHOULD. IN THE NAME OF JESUS I PRAY. AMEN.

---

[1] Exodus 15:11; Psalm 99:9; Isaiah 6:1-3; Revelation 4:8.
[2] Deuteronomy 32:4; Jeremiah 9:23-24; Revelation 15:3.
[3] Psalm 97:1-2; Psalm 119:137; Jeremiah 23:6.
[4] Exodus 20:19.
[5] Jeremiah 31:3; John 3:16; Romans 5:8.
[6] Ephesians 2:4; James 5:11; 1 Peter 1:3.
[7] Ephesians 2:8; Hebrews 4:16; 1 Peter 5:10.
[8] Hebrews 2:14-18; Hebrews 4:15-16.
[9] Isaiah 53:4-10,12.
[10] Romans 5:8.
[11] A.W. Tozer, *The Knowledge of the Holy* quoted in *Disciplines for the Inner Life* by Bob Benson and Michael W. Benson (Waco: Word Books Publisher, 1985), p. 3.

CHAPTER 2

THE TRUTH ABOUT SALVATION

Once we know the truth about God we begin to understand the truth about our salvation and the Source of our security. Contrary to a common misconception, our righteousness is not based on our personal performance but on the finished work of Jesus Christ. His sinless life has been imputed to us; therefore, His righteousness has become our righteousness, His valor our valor.

The Bible calls this justification. Romans 5:18-19 says, "...just as the result of one trespass was condemnation for all men, so also the result of one act of righteousness was justification that brings life for all men. For just as through the disobedience of the one man the many were made sinners, so also through the obedience of the one man the many will be made righteous."

Here's how it works: "God made him [Jesus] who had no sin to be sin for us, so that in him we might become the righteousness of God."[1]

How was Jesus, Who was God incarnate, made to "be sin for us"? By committing sin? Hardly! He was "...tempted in every way, just as we are—yet was without sin."[2]

The Sinless One was made to be sin for us by an act of God!

God took the sinfulness of fallen humanity and imputed it to Jesus. With that sovereign act, our sinfulness became His sinfulness, our "sin" (or who we were, our fallen nature) became Who He was— "God made him who had no sin to be sin...."[3]

How then do we become "the righteousness of God"? By living sinless lives? By walking in personal righteousness? Of course not! Jesus was not made sin by sinning, and we are not made righteous by our good works. It is an act of God! When we express faith in the finished work of Jesus Christ, God imputes to us the righteousness of Christ. And we who were not righteous are made the righteousness of God in Him. "All this is God's doing...."[4]

To more fully understand what we are talking about let me distinguish between *justification* and *sanctification*. Simply put, in layman's terms, *justification* refers to our right standing before God, while *sanctification* refers to our daily walk with Him. Justification is what Christ has done for us (on the Cross). Sanctification is what Christ is doing in us. Our justification is a finished work. Positionally, we are men of valor.[5] Our sanctification is a continuing work. Experientially, we are becoming men of valor. Hebrews 10:14 addresses both issues. "...by one sacrifice he [Jesus] has made perfect [justified] forever those who are being made holy [sanctified]."

Positionally, we have been made perfect forever. Experientially, we are being made holy—that is, we are in the process of being sanctified; we are in the process of living out what we already are positionally.

Positionally, we are complete in Christ at the moment of conversion.[6] Our righteousness is perfect because it is the righteousness of God.[7] As long as we remain in relationship with Christ Jesus through faith in His finished work on the Cross our positional standing does not change. It does not improve, no matter how valiantly we live, for it is already perfect. Nor is it threatened when we fail, as we are all prone to do, for it is not based on our personal performance. It is dependent on nothing but our faith in the finished work of Christ—that is, what He has done for us!

Experientially, however, we are babies in Christ, not only when we receive Him as our Savior, but if we don't "grow up" in our salvation.[8] Paul writes, "Brothers, I could not address you as spiritual but as worldly—mere infants in Christ."[9] And as immature believers, we continue to react with carnal attitudes and self-centered desires. We fall prey to temptation and become ensnared in the things of the world.

On the experiential level then, while we are a "new creation" in Christ,[10] there is not necessarily an immediate corresponding Christlikeness in our daily lives. Experientially, we are in the process of becoming what we already are positionally. This is Christ's continuing work in us. And like Paul we are "...confident of this, that he who began a good work in [us] will carry it on to completion...."[11]

When a man sees God as a merciful heavenly Father, Who has made perfect provision for his salvation, he is free to come before Him, totally transparent and completely honest. Since his right standing with God is based on the finished work of Christ and not his own performance, he need not fear being rejected. And freed from the fear of rejection, he can honestly acknowledge his deep need and receive the grace of God that both redeems and renews.

ACTION STEPS:

▼ IS YOUR SECURITY IN YOUR PERSONAL WALK—YOUR DEVOTIONAL LIFE, YOUR CHURCH ATTENDANCE, AND YOUR CHRISTIAN SERVICE—OR IS IT IN THE FINISHED WORK OF JESUS CHRIST?

▼ IF YOU ARE TRUSTING IN YOURSELF RATHER THAN IN THE FINISHED WORK OF JESUS CHRIST, WHAT STEPS ARE YOU GOING TO TAKE TO CHANGE? BE SPECIFIC.

THOUGHT FOR THE DAY:

"In the arc of my unremarkable life, wherein the victories have been small and personal, the trials fairly pedestrian, and the failures large enough to deeply wound me and those I love, I have repeated endlessly the pattern of falling down and getting up, falling down and getting up. Each time I fall, I am propelled to renew my efforts by a blind trust in the forgiveness of my sins from sheer grace, in the acquittal, vindication, and justification of my ragged journey based not on any good deeds I have done (the approach taken by the Pharisee in the temple) but on an unflagging trust in the love of a gracious and merciful God."[12]

Brennan Manning

SCRIPTURE FOR THE DAY:

The LORD is compassionate and gracious,
slow to anger, abounding in love.
He will not always accuse,
nor will he harbor his anger forever;
he does not treat us as our sins deserve
or repay us according to our iniquities.
For as high as the heavens are above the earth,
so great is his love for those who fear him;
as far as the east is from the west,
so far has he removed our transgressions from us.

—PSALM 103:8-12

PRAYER:

LORD, FREE ME FROM MY INORDINATE NEED TO MEASURE UP.
TEACH ME TO TRUST ONLY IN THE FINISHED WORK OF
JESUS CHRIST MY SAVIOR EVEN AS I YIELD MYSELF TO
HIS CONTINUING WORK IN ME. IN THE NAME OF JESUS I PRAY. AMEN.

[1] 2 Corinthians 5:21.
[2] Hebrews 4:15.
[3] 2 Corinthians 5:21.
[4] 2 Corinthians 5:18 PHILLIPS.
[5] See Judges 6:1-12.
[6] Colossians 2:10 NKJV.
[7] 2 Corinthians 5:21.
[8] 1 Peter 2:2.
[9] 1 Corinthians 3:1.
[10] 2 Corinthians 5:17.
[11] Philippians 1:6.
[12] Brennan Manning, *Ruthless Trust the Ragamuffin's Path to God* (San Francisco: HarperSanFrancisco, 2000), p. 12.

CHAPTER 3

THE TRUTH ABOUT OURSELVES

Elijah is the most revered prophet in Israel's long history, a valiant man if ever there was one. Yet he reached a point in his life when he became suicidal. He was so depressed that he prayed to die.[1]

Undoubtedly, there were a number of contributing factors, including (but not limited to) unrealistic expectations, physical and emotional exhaustion, as well as years of isolation. Still, the primary cause may have been his relationship with God, which appears to have been built on power rather than intimacy, performance rather than relationship.

God began the restoration process by giving Elijah a spiritual experience based on intimacy rather than power, a gentle whisper rather than a roaring wind.[2] Why? Because power is seldom what we need when we have come to the end of ourselves. At those times, we need relationship—a gentle whisper assuring us of our value, of our place in God's kingdom, "a still small voice" telling us of His love, of our value to Him.

If you've ever had an experience like that, you know why Elijah covered his face when he heard the still small voice of God. (v. 13.) The thing you have longed for, searched for your whole life, is finally happening—and in the most unexpected way, when you least deserve it. Jesus is there, with you, nearer than the breath you breathe, more real than life itself.

Your heart cries out to Him: "Whisper to me, Jesus, because my heart is heavy. Whisper to me, Jesus, because discouragement has taken me by the throat. Whisper to me, Jesus, because I am alone and undone on the inside. Whisper to me, Jesus, because I can't bear to live another moment without You."

And then He whispers things so sweet, so holy, so tender, it seems your heart will burst. He whispers things so real, so true, so eternal, that you have to cover your face. His presence is so pure you can't bear to look, and yet you must. You must, for this is the moment for which you've lived your whole life; the moment when, finally, you are brought face-to-face with Him.

Once we have been assured of God's love, of our value to Him, and of our place in His kingdom, then He begins to address the root cause of our spiritual crisis. "...Then a voice said to him, 'What are you doing here, Elijah?'"[3]

This is the moment of truth for Elijah, and for us! The question really isn't "What are you doing here?" but more precisely "Who are you? What kind of person are you? What choices have you made that brought you to this moment?"

God raises these questions, not because He doesn't know, but to bring us face-to-face with the truth about ourselves. In fact, God knows everything about us; nothing is hid from His eyes. Of Jeremiah He said, "Before I formed you in the womb I knew you...."[4] Jesus declared, "'...God knows your hearts....'"[5]

Yet what is so obvious to God is often hid from our eyes. We once saw it clearly, but over the years we have learned to edit the truth about ourselves until it is more to our liking. It isn't an outright lie so much as it is a change in perception. The "facts" remain the same, but the conclusions are totally different. We have mastered the subtle art of deception, and tragically, we have become victims of our own deceit.

God brings us to such moments, not to humiliate us, but to set us free. As long as we believe the deception we have created about ourselves, we are a prisoner of that lie. We can have only the most superficial relationship with Him, and others, because the self we bring to the relationship is a false self. In truth, we are not relating to one another, but rather building an elaborate masquerade.

To face the truth about ourselves means to see ourselves as God sees us—no more duplicity or self-deception. Thus, when Elijah stands in the presence of God, he is able, at last, to confront his deepest feelings. Until now he has been unwilling to acknowledge them, let alone examine them, for he is sure that they are not the kind of feelings a prophet ought to have. But now, standing in the circle of God's unconditional love, hearing the gentle whisper of His affirmation, he finds the courage to face his secret fears and inner demons.

Such fearless self-honesty is not possible apart from the presence of God. To see ourselves as we truly are, with all our selfishness and carnality, would be devastating were it not for the grace of God[6] that shows us what we are destined to be in Him—men of valor. Even as we cringe at the revelation of our unabashed carnality, our shameless self-interest, He gives us a glimpse, in His Word and by His still small voice, of what we can be in Christ Jesus. And this vision of our transformed self, coupled with the holy presence of the Lord, gives us the faith and the courage to face the truth about ourselves. And as we face the truth, He sets us free from the past and from our deluded self to become the men of valor He has called us to be.

ACTION STEPS:

▼ AS YOU READ THIS CHAPTER, WHAT THOUGHTS AND FEELINGS DID YOU HAVE? BE HONEST AND BE SPECIFIC.

▼ IF GOD REVEALED SOME AREAS IN YOUR LIFE THAT NEED ADDRESSING, HOW ARE YOU GOING TO DEAL WITH THEM? BE SPECIFIC.

THOUGHT FOR THE DAY:

"The process (of spiritual growth) is like watching the growth of a child. If one is with them each day it will be hard to see them growing. It is only as we measure them against a mark on the doorpost or try to fit them into last spring's clothes that we realize the extent of their growth. And even though the process may be imperceptible to us at a given moment we will begin to note by reading back through our journal or by sensing our responses and attitudes in everyday matters and relationships that He is changing us and endowing us with the fruits of His Spirit."[7]

Bob Benson and Michael W. Benson

SCRIPTURES FOR THE DAY:
Search me, O God, and know my heart;
test me and know my anxious thoughts.
See if there is any offensive way in me,
and lead me in the way everlasting.

PSALM 139:23-24

The lamp of the LORD searches the spirit of a man;
it searches out his inmost being.

PROVERBS 20:27

☩

PRAYER:

LORD, ENABLE ME TO SEE MYSELF AS YOU SEE ME. REVEAL
THE SELFISHNESS I CANNOT SEE, THE MATERIALISM I'VE OVERLOOKED,
AND THE PRIDE I'M UNAWARE OF, BUT DON'T STOP THERE. SHOW ME
THE MAN I CAN BE, THE MAN YOU ARE REMAKING IN THE IMAGE OF
YOUR DEAR SON—A MAN OF VALOR. IN JESUS NAME I PRAY. AMEN.

---

[1] 1 Kings 19:4.
[2] 1 Kings 19:8-12.
[3] 1 Kings 19:13.
[4] Jeremiah 1:5.
[5] Luke 16:15.
[6] 1 Corinthains 15:10; 2 Corinthians 12:9
[7] Bob Benson and Michael W. Benson, *Disciplines for the Inner Life* (Waco: Word Books, 1985), p. 224.

CHAPTER 4

SPIRITUAL DISCIPLINES
FOR MEN OF VALOR[1]

Being a man of valor is both a gift and a discipline. It is a gift in the sense that God has given every man the capacity for greatness. It is a discipline in the sense that, although God will empower you,[2] it is up to you to exercise the spiritual disciplines that will enable you to become the man God intends you to be. There are four disciplines that are absolutely critical for those who wish to be men of valor—prayer, journaling, Bible study, and fasting.

Many men approach these spiritual disciplines with unrealistic expectations. They expect instant results—instant insight into the scriptures; instant awareness of God's presence; instant increase in their faith; instant victory over the weaknesses of their flesh. Not infrequently, what they get is instant disappointment. When their expectations are not realized instantly, they may become disillusioned.

A productive devotional life is built on consistent discipline. There will be times when you are blessed with a sense of divine presence. At other times the Word of God will open unto you in a special way, and spiritual insight into the scriptures will quicken your understanding. There may even be times when you experience a special manifestation of the sanctifying power of the Holy Spirit, times when the habits of your flesh fall away, but these are the exception rather than the rule. On the whole, the devotional life is more discipline than inspiration. And it is consistent discipline that prepares us for those times of special visitation.

As you prepare for the devotional life, it is important to approach it realistically. The amount of time you commit yourself to should be something you can expect to be faithful to each day. Start with ten minutes—not an hour. If you decided to take up running, you wouldn't begin with the Boston Marathon. You would probably start with a graduated training program, working up to longer distances over a period of time. Use that same principle for your devotional life.

Much of your devotional time will be discipline without immediate or obvious benefits. Do not let that discourage you. Consider the analogy of the runner again. Early in his training his running is pure drudgery; sometimes it is closer to sheer torture. His muscles get sore, his feet hurt, sometimes he gets blisters or shin splints; but over a period of weeks, his body rounds into shape. Without realizing it he starts to feel better. Even after he is in shape there will be days when he has to force himself to run. As often as not the actual act of running is more discipline than pleasure.

So it is with the devotional life. The spiritual benefits are seldom immediately apparent. Sometimes after days of Bible study and prayer, you may feel no closer to God. It may seem as if you are making no progress. Don't give up. Like the runner, your spiritual man is slowly rounding into shape.

Marathoners talk of "breaking through the wall." They run until they are on the verge of collapsing. By sheer determination they press on, and suddenly they are through the wall—they get their second wind—but it's more than that. They experience an almost euphoric feeling, a runner's high. That experience corresponds with those times in our devotional life when we are literally overwhelmed with the presence of God. It does not happen every time we pray or read the Scriptures, but when it does, it makes everything—all the discipline, all the solitude and sacrifice, all the hours of waiting—worthwhile.

ACTION STEPS:

▼ IF YOU DO NOT ALREADY HAVE A REGULAR DEVOTIONAL TIME, MAKE A COMMITMENT TO ESTABLISH ONE. SET ASIDE TIME EACH DAY TO BE ALONE WITH GOD. READ THE SCRIPTURES, PRAY, AND JOURNAL.

▼ CONSIDER PARTNERING WITH ANOTHER MAN TO MOTIVATE YOU TO BE CONSISTENT.

▼ MAKE FASTING A REGULAR PART OF YOUR SPIRITUAL DISCIPLINES.

THOUGHT FOR THE DAY:

"We will never get anywhere in life without discipline, be it in the arts, business, athletics, or academics. This is doubly so in spiritual matters. In other areas we may be able to claim some innate advantage. An athlete may be born with a strong body, a musician with perfect pitch, or an artist with an eye for perspective. But none of us can claim an innate spiritual advantage. In reality, we are all equally disadvantaged....Therefore, as children of grace, our spiritual discipline is everything—everything!"[3]

R. Kent Hughes

SCRIPTURE FOR THE DAY:

...train yourself to be godly. For physical training is of some value,
but godliness has value for all things, holding promise
for both the present life and the life to come.

1 TIMOTHY 4:7-8

✠

PRAYER:

LORD, MANY OF US ARE NOT DISCIPLINED MEN BY NATURE.
WE EAT TOO MUCH AND EXERCISE TOO LITTLE. WE STAY UP
TOO LATE AND HAVE A DREADFUL HABIT OF HITTING THE SNOOZE
BUTTON TWO OR THREE TIMES EACH MORNING. WORST OF ALL WE
ARE NOT FAITHFUL TO OUR QUIET TIME. FORGIVE OUR PAST FAILURES.
BY YOUR GRACE, WE WILL DO BETTER, WE WILL BE DISCIPLINED MEN,
ESPECIALLY WHERE IT CONCERNS OUR DEVOTIONAL LIFE. AMEN.

---

[1]   Much of the material in this chapter is based on material in: Richard Exley, *Deliver Me* (Nashville: Thomas Nelson Publishers, 1998), pp. 258, 259.

[2]   2 Corinthians 12:9.

[3]   R. Kent Hughes, *Disciplines of a Godly Man* (Wheaton: Crossway Books, 1991), p. 15.

CHAPTER 5

THE DISCIPLINE OF DEVOTIONAL PRAYER

What breath is to the body prayer is to the soul. It restores our spiritual vitality. It reshapes us into God's image. It brings our thoughts and feelings into perfect accord with the Father's desires, and enables us to think God's thoughts after Him. It enlarges our vision. It puts all of life into perspective and brings eternity into focus.

There are several important dimensions of prayer for a man of valor—devotional prayer, intercessory prayer, and spiritual warfare—but because of the scope of this chapter, we are focusing on devotional praying only. By its very nature devotional praying focuses on the inner life. It allows the Spirit to address those issues that are preventing us from being fully conformed to the image of Christ.[1]

By focusing on matters of the heart, devotional praying helps us become the man God has called us to be. Of course, we are not talking about morbid introspection but the sanctifying work of the Holy Spirit. He moves us to examine ourselves and our relationships in light of God's Holy Word.

The way a man interacts with others reflects the character of his inner man, as light and heat are manifestations of fire. In the crucible of interpersonal relationships, the nature of his heart is made known. In moments of pressure or confrontation, his true self is revealed. Unfortunately many a man dismisses these experiences without examining their roots or what they reveal about his spiritual life. Well might he remember that Jesus said, "...out of the overflow of the heart the mouth speaks. The good man brings good things out of the good stored up in him, and the evil man brings evil things out of the evil stored up in him."[2]

Although a man can be tempted in any way at any time, as he matures in the Lord the nature of his temptations tend to change. Early in his spiritual walk his temptations are generally the more obvious temptations of the flesh—lust, ambition, and materialism. But as he grows in the Lord, they often become the more subtle temptations of the heart.

How, you may be wondering, does a man go about developing the kind of spiritual understanding that allows him to overcome these inner enemies? First, you must make a commitment to this kind of devotional praying. You must see it as a spiritual discipline necessary to your personal growth and wholeness. If you think of it in any other way, it becomes optional—good but not absolutely necessary.

Next, you must set aside time on a regular basis—daily is best— to wait before the Lord. As you wait before Him, you should consciously present the circumstances and relationships of your life to Him for examination.[3] Be sensitive to the thoughts and impressions you receive. These are often insights from the Lord to move us to repentance and growth.

Finally, act on the things the Lord is revealing to you. His grace will enable you to make whatever changes He is impressing upon your heart. If you are in doubt regarding the appropriate response, seek the counsel of a spiritually mature brother in the Lord. Remember, obedience produces life-giving change, while disobedience hardens the heart.

ACTION STEPS:

▼ EXAMINE YOUR PRAYER LIFE. ARE YOUR PRAYERS DEVOTIONAL— FOCUSING ON YOUR PERSONAL SPIRITUAL DEVELOPMENT? OR ARE THEY MORE PETITIONARY IN NATURE—FOCUSING ON YOUR DESIRES, WANTS, AND NEEDS?

▼ IF THEY TEND TO BE MOSTLY PETITIONARY, DISCIPLINE YOURSELF TO INCLUDE DEVOTIONAL PRAYING AS A PART OF YOUR DAILY PRAYER TIME.

▼ AS YOU LOOK BACK OVER YOUR PRAYER TIME THE PAST SEVERAL DAYS, WHAT HAS GOD BEEN SHOWING YOU? BE SPECIFIC.

THOUGHT FOR THE DAY:

"Prayer is like a time exposure to God. Our souls function like photographic plates, and Christ's shining image is the light. The more we expose our lives to the white-hot sun of His righteous life (for say, five, ten, fifteen, thirty minutes, or an hour a day), the more His image will be burned into our character—His love, His compassion, His truth, His integrity, His humility."[4]

R. Kent Hughes

SCRIPTURE FOR THE DAY:

You are my portion, O LORD;
I have promised to obey your words.
I have sought your face with all my heart;
be gracious to me according to your promise.
I have considered my ways
and have turned my steps to your statutes.
I will hasten and not delay
to obey your commands.

PSALM 119:57-60

✠

PRAYER:

LORD, I'M SO IMPRESSIONABLE. I SO QUICKLY ASSIMILATE THE ATTITUDES, THE CHARACTERISTICS, AND THE PHILOSOPHIES OF THE WORLD AROUND ME. THAT'S WHY I SO DESPERATELY NEED THIS TIME TO BE WITH YOU. LET ME BE IMPRESSIONABLE NOW. SUPERIMPOSE YOUR MIND UPON MINE; MAKE MY NATURE AND PERSONALITY UNMISTAKABLY LIKE YOURS. LEAVE ME FOREVER MARKED WITH THIS MEETING, STAMPED INDELIBLY WITH THE EVIDENCE OF YOUR PRESENCE. AMEN.

---

[1] See Romans 8:29 and Galatians 4:19.
[2] Matthew 12:34-35.
[3] See Psalm 139:23-24.
[4] R. Kent Hughes, *Disciplines of a Godly Man* (Wheaton: Crossway Books: A Division of Good News Publishers, 1991), p. 81.

CHAPTER 6

THE DISCIPLINE OF JOURNALING

Journaling is a historical spiritual discipline and the keeping of personal journals has played a significant role in the history of the Church. From St. Augustine to Pascal to the Religious Society of Friends (Quakers), some form of the spiritual journal has been used for spiritual discipline and growth.

Personal experience has shown me that there are several advantages to journaling. First, it is a discipline that encourages me to prayerfully examine all the issues of my life. This is important because left to my own devices I will generally try to avoid those issues or relationships that are painful. Even when I pray about them, I usually just offer some kind of generic prayer—something like, "Heal this relationship" or "Resolve this difficulty." When I journal I am forced to think about them deeply and prayerfully.

Journaling also forces me to be specific. When I put pen to paper I have to come to grips with my elusive thoughts and feelings. The written word allows no vague generalities. It demands that I identify what I am feeling and why. For instance, some years ago I found myself dealing with a lot of anger. In an attempt to get things into perspective, I turned to my journal. After writing out my thoughts and feelings in detail, I discovered that much of my anger had nothing to do with the current situation. Instead, I realized it was the product of little hurts, carefully kept—sometimes for years—which would suddenly explode in the most inappropriate ways. The issue that finally triggered my outburst was usually a legitimate concern, but it was soon lost in the outpouring of my wrath.

Thankfully the Lord is doing a sanctifying work in me and I am no longer the angry man I once was. Still, I doubt if I could have overcome my anger without the insights provided through the discipline of journaling.

Finally, journaling helps me put things into perspective. Well has it been said, "If [we] can write things out [we] can see them, and they are not trapped within [our] own subjectivity...."[1]

"Not long ago," writes Madeleine L'Engle, "someone I love said something which wounded me grievously, and I was desolate that this person could have made such a comment to me. So, in great pain, I crawled to my journal and wrote it all out in a great burst of self-pity. And when I had set it down, when I had it before me, I saw that something I myself had said had called forth the words which had hurt me so. It had, in fact, been my own fault. But I would never have seen it if I had not written it out."[2]

Don't kid yourself. It's not only women who sometimes lack perspective. Men do too. We often have only the vaguest understanding of an experience or situation—until we discipline ourselves to write it down. Once we put pen to paper, our elusive thoughts and feelings seem to crystallize enabling us to present our true situation to God for healing and growth.

ACTION STEPS:

▼ IF YOU DO NOT ALREADY PRACTICE THE DISCIPLINE OF JOURNALING, MAKE A COMMITMENT TO DO SO NOW. GO TO A BOOKSTORE OR OFFICE SUPPLY STORE AND PURCHASE A JOURNAL. IF YOU ARE MORE COMFORTABLE USING A COMPUTER, YOU CAN PURCHASE A JOURNAL PROGRAM FOR YOUR COMPUTER.

▼ DURING YOUR QUIET TIME BE SENSITIVE TO THE THOUGHTS AND IMPRESSIONS YOU ARE RECEIVING. RECORD THEM IN YOUR JOURNAL. THIS IS OFTEN THE WAY THE LORD SPEAKS TO US. BE ESPECIALLY SENSITIVE TO THOSE THOUGHTS THAT RELATE TO DECISIONS YOU MUST MAKE OR THE RELATIONSHIPS IN WHICH YOU FIND YOURSELF.

▼ IF YOU ARE ALREADY JOURNALING, GO BACK AND READ THE ENTRIES YOU HAVE MADE DURING THE PAST WEEKS AND MONTHS TO REMIND YOURSELF OF WHAT THE LORD HAS BEEN DOING IN YOUR LIFE.

THOUGHT FOR THE DAY:

"Keeping a journal is the process of digesting the spiritual meaning of the events of each day. These events have come with rapidity; they have come with feeling, some with thinking, some with just doing. Sometime during your hurried day you must take time out to reflect on the deeper significance of these events and to digest them into your own 'life-sustaining milk.' As you make sense of them, you will put them in perspective of their importance and lasting value to your own life."[3]

Robert Wood

SCRIPTURES FOR THE DAY:

The LORD *called Samuel a third time, and Samuel got up and went to Eli and said, "Here I am; you called me." Then Eli realized that the* LORD *was calling the boy. So Eli told Samuel, "Go and lie down, and if he calls you, say, 'Speak,* LORD, *for your servant is listening.'" So Samuel went and lay down in his place. The* LORD *came and stood there, calling as at the other times, "Samuel! Samuel!" Then Samuel said, "Speak, for your servant is listening."*

1 SAMUEL 3:8-10

His [Jesus'] mother said to the servants, "Do whatever he tells you."

JOHN 2:5

PRAYER:

LORD, THINGS HAPPEN SO QUICKLY THAT I SELDOM

TAKE THE TIME TO REFLECT ON THEIR SPIRITUAL SIGNIFICANCE.

HELP ME TO SLOW DOWN SO I CAN HEAR YOUR VOICE AND OBEY. AMEN.

[1] Madeleine L'Engle, *Walking On Water* (Wheaton: Harold Shaw Publishers, 1980).
[2] Ibid.
[3] Robert Wood, *A Thirty-day Experiment in Prayer* (Nashville: The Upper Room, 1978), p. 9.

CHAPTER 7

THE DISCIPLINE OF SCRIPTURE [1]

To the subjective disciplines of prayer and journaling, we add the objective discipline of study, especially the study of God's Word. Even as we study the Word, we remind ourselves that it is bread to be eaten, not literature to be admired. We continually put it into practice, letting it change and shape us.

When we read the Bible devotionally, we do so on at least three levels. By that I mean we read it in order to answer three questions. First, *What is the historical setting; what did this passage of Scripture mean to the person who wrote it, and what did it mean to his contemporary who read it?* Reading on this level preserves the Scripture's objectivity, its historical perspective. It also focuses its meaning for us—the twenty-first century reader.

The second question is, *What does this passage say about God?* I am told that in the Library of Congress there is a copy of the United States Constitution, which when viewed from a certain angle, seems to bear a portrait of George Washington, the father of our country. So it is with the Scriptures. When we read them with faith, they are more than just a collection of ancient poetry or proverbs; they are a revelation of God Himself, a portrait of our Heavenly Father.

Not long ago my Bible reading took me into several days of lengthy genealogies. One morning in exasperation I prayed, "Lord, what is the meaning of all these names?" I didn't expect an answer, but suddenly a thought sprang full-blown into my mind. It seemed God was saying, "I am a personal God and every individual is important to me. Every time you read a genealogy, I am reminding you that I know your name, as well as the names of your parents and grandparents."

Needless to say, I will never read the genealogies in Scripture the same way again. Now every time I read them I will be reminded that God is a personal God and that He knows me and is involved in every aspect of my life. By asking the question, "What does this passage say about God?" I came to a fuller understanding and appreciation of His character.

The third question is more personal: *What does this passage say to me about my spiritual condition, about my life and my standing with God?* The Bible is a living book[2] that transcends time and place. God uses it to speak directly into our individual situations. Read it to receive a word from Him.

Several years ago I was going through a difficult time. I seemed to have reached a stalemate in my life and ministry. After several years of remarkable growth, the church I was serving seemed to reach a plateau. No matter what I did we seemed stuck. To complicate matters a small, but vocal group, were critical of my leadership. On top of everything else, my writing was not going very well. As a result, I was experiencing some doubts regarding the effectiveness of my ministry.

One morning during my devotional time, I was reading in the Psalms when I came across Psalm 138:7-8. Although I had read that passage numerous times before, that particular morning the words seemed to leap off the page. "Though I walk in the midst of trouble, you preserve my life; you stretch out your hand against the anger of my foes, with your right hand you save me. The LORD will fulfill his purpose for me; your love, O LORD, endures forever—do not abandon the works of your hands."

Although the situation did not immediately change, I was at peace. God had spoken to me through His Word. No matter what others did He would fulfill His purpose in my life! Not necessarily my dreams and goals, but His purpose—and that was enough.

Finally, when you read the Scriptures, act on what you are learning. Put it into practice; let it change your life. As Richard Foster says, "When we come to the Scripture we come to be changed, not to amass information."[3]

ACTION STEPS:

▼ IN YOUR JOURNAL, OR ON A 3 X 5 INDEX CARD, WRITE OUT YOUR COMMITMENT TO READ THE BIBLE FAITHFULLY. YOUR COMMITMENT SHOULD FOCUS ON FAITHFULNESS—DAILY BIBLE READING—RATHER THAN ON THE AMOUNT YOU READ EACH DAY.

▼ ASK YOUR PASTOR OR A MATURE SPIRITUAL BROTHER TO HELP YOU FIND A BIBLE READING PROGRAM THAT WILL ENABLE YOU TO READ THROUGH THE ENTIRE BIBLE.

▼ MAKE YOURSELF ACCOUNTABLE TO YOUR PASTOR OR A MATURE SPIRITUAL BROTHER.

THOUGHT FOR THE DAY:

"The voice of God heard through the Scriptures, comes to us through human hands with many cultural and historical distortions. Some readers get hung up on the history, or the scholarship, or the customs and miss the whole point. But for those readers who want to know God, who want to hear His voice, He is there!

"A Chinese Christian once said, 'Reading the Bible is like eating fish—you have to watch out for the bones.' When you come to something you do not understand, set it aside, like a fish bone, and go on. You would not throw out the whole fish because of a few bones, so do not throw out the Bible just because you cannot understand it all."[4]

Richard Exley

SCRIPTURE FOR THE DAY:

I rejoice in following your statutes
as one rejoices in great riches.
I meditate on your precepts
and consider your ways.
I delight in your decrees;
I will not neglect your word.

PSALM 119:14-16

PRAYER:

LORD, FORGIVE ME FOR ALL THE TIMES I HAVE ALLOWED THE DISTRACTIONS OF LIFE TO CAUSE ME TO NEGLECT YOUR WORD. GIVE ME THE GRACE AND THE DISCIPLINE TO LIVE IN YOUR WORD DAY BY DAY AND THUS RENEW MY LIFE. HELP ME TO MEMORIZE IT, TO HIDE IT IN MY HEART THAT I MIGHT NOT SIN AGAINST YOU. IN YOUR HOLY NAME I PRAY. AMEN.

---

[1]   Much of the material in this chapter is based on material in: Richard Exley, *Deliver Me* (Nashville: Thomas Nelson Publishers, 1998), pp. 259, 260.

[2]   Hebrews 4:12-13.

[3]   Richard J. Foster, *The Celebration of Discipline* (San Francisco: Harper and Row, 1978), p. 60.

[4]   Richard Exley, *Deliver Me,* (Nashville: Thomas Nelson Publishers, 1998) p. 260.

CHAPTER 8

THE DISCIPLINE OF DEVOTIONAL READING

A good book renews us in a way nothing else can. I'm not talking about weighty books that tax the mind, but insightful books that touch a man's soul—books that give him a glimpse of life in all its poignancy and passion. Books that put him in touch with God and his own life experience. Any book that can do that is worth whatever it costs and more.

Not long ago I read a book that did just that for me—*Things Unseen* by Mark Buchanan. After reading just a few pages, I knew I had discovered a treasure. The content was sound and thought provoking, the author's style captivating, and his use of language fresh. Soon I found myself swept along by the sheer power of his words and the images they invoked.

In one section, he wrote about his father's anger and the emotional toll it took on the family:

"Something goes wrong. I don't remember what. The toast burns, or the coffee spills, or something breaks. In the huge shuddering silence that follows, I brace myself for anger, shouting, accusation...."[1]

I could read no further, for in telling his story Mark had written my own. Only I was not the frightened boy huddling in the corner. I was the angry father, or I should say that I used to be the angry father.

For years my anger and my moods hovered just beneath the surface, ready to erupt and terrorize my family at the slightest provocation. Worst of all, I never even realized it. Though God's grace has healed me and the tragic wounds my anger inflicted on my wife and daughter, anything that sparks a painful reminder of those dark days is sure to touch a shamed and grieving place deep inside of me.

Yet, that is not the whole of it, for if all I were made to remember were my angry failings, I would have surely slammed the book shut in disgust. No, it was not fear and anger that *Things Unseen* called forth, but light and laughter. Anger was just the backdrop Buchanan used for the gem of forgiveness, and even in my darkest moments, that's what I hungered for—the light of forgiveness.

"But my parents laugh...." That's what Buchanan writes—"But my parents laugh." Instead of anger the cabin is filled with laughter, and in his father's laughter, Mark finds healing and hope.

"In that laughter, in the clean, deep, wide-openness of it, all things are possible...That laughter is a sign as consoling as a fig branch in a dove's beak, a promise as dazzling as a rainbow arched over a world washed fresh. It is a pledge that the earth will not be destroyed as before."[2]

Now I am laughing too, and crying as well, for like Mark's father I have been forgiven. I have been set free from the angry demons within. No longer do I terrorize those I love. Laughter—sometimes hardly more than a soft chuckle, sometimes a sidesplitting belly laugh—has replaced the bitter recriminations of the past. Once more I am reminded of how wonderful life is when the light of God's love bursts into our brokenness, making all things new.

Only God knows how many books He has used to touch me, change me, and make me into the man He has called me to be. Some of the more memorable ones are, *A Touch of Wonder* by Arthur Gordon; *Tuesdays with Morrie* by Mitch Albom; *Tracks of a Fellow Struggler* by John Claypool; *Windows of the Soul* by Ken Gire Jr.; *Six Hours One Friday* by Max Lucado; *Telling the Truth* by Frederick Buechner; and *A Song I Knew by Heart* by Bret Lott.

The books that speak to you may not be the same ones that speak to me. That's okay. The important thing is that you find books that nourish your soul and call you to new life in Christ. Depending on the seasons of your life and your personal spiritual development, the books that appeal to you will likely vary. On more than one occasion, I have started reading a highly recommended book only to lay it aside in frustration after a chapter or two. Was the book overrated or poorly written? Maybe, but more likely the problem was my own. Perhaps I was not spiritually or emotionally ready for that particular book. Sometimes I will return to the same book a year or two later and find that I cannot put it down. I am in a different season of life and now my soul literally resonates with the author's message.

Books will minister to you in ways nothing else can. They will introduce you to people you will never meet any other way. They will take you to places to which you will never travel. They will enlarge your thinking and expand your vision. They will renew your mind and refresh your soul. In truth, reading a book by an author whose heart and mind are steeped in God's eternal truth is like sitting at the feet of a truly wise man. His writings are a fountain of life (Proverbs 13:14).

ACTION STEPS:

▼ ASK YOUR PASTOR OR A MAN YOU RESPECT TO RECOMMEND BOOKS FOR YOU TO READ.

▼ MAKE READING A PART OF YOUR DAILY QUIET TIME.

▼ CARRY A BOOK WITH YOU AT ALL TIMES AND READ AT EVERY OPPORTUNITY.

THOUGHT FOR THE DAY:

"Stories give us eyes other than our own with which to see the world...The power of story is in the way it incarnates ideas, putting flesh and blood on skeletal principles. If you want to understand the dangers of ambition, for example, to understand it in a way that will impact you the rest of your life, read *The Thornbirds*. If you want to see the devastation of adultery in a way that will shake you, see the movie *Camelot*.

When we see such stories, with all their hardships, colors, and juices, they move us not by external forces but by internal ones. Not by law but by grace. By the quickening of our conscience and the stirrings of our heart."[3]

Ken Gire Jr.

☩

SCRIPTURE FOR THE DAY:

With many similar parables Jesus spoke the word to them, as much as they could understand. He did not say anything to them without using a parable.

MARK 4:33-34

✠

PRAYER:

LORD, THANK YOU FOR ALL OF THE BOOKS THAT HAVE ENRICHED ME. THANK YOU FOR THE MEN AND WOMEN WHO POURED THEIR LIVES INTO THE WRITING OF THEM. BLESS AND ANOINT EACH OF THEM. MAY THEIR FAITHFULNESS TO THE GIFTS YOU HAVE GIVEN THEM CONTINUE TO PRODUCE BOOKS THAT BECOME TOOLS IN YOUR HANDS TO MAKE US INTO MEN OF VALOR. AMEN.

[1] Mark Buchanan, *Things Unseen* (Sisters, OR: Multnomah Publishers, Inc., 2002), p. 16.
[2] Ibid.
[3] Ken Gire, Jr., *Windows of the Soul* (Grand Rapids: Zondervan Publishing House, 1996), p. 76.

CHAPTER 9

THE DISCIPLINE
OF FASTING

The fourth discipline for men of valor is fasting. Although we do not usually give fasting the same attention we give prayer and Bible reading, the Scriptures put it in the same category. In His teaching on fasting in Matthew 6, Jesus did not say "if" you fast, but "when" you fast.[1] The inference is clear—there should be times of regular fasting in our lives just as there are times of regular prayer. Unfortunately many men operate under the assumption that there is no need to fast unless they receive special spiritual direction or they are facing a major crisis.

The Scriptures identify several types of fasts. First, there is a normal fast, which means to abstain from all foods, solid or liquid, but not water. This is most likely the type of fast that Jesus went on. Luke says, "...He ate nothing during those [forty] days, and at the end of them he was hungry."[2]

A second type of fast is an absolute fast, which means to abstain not only from eating, but also from drinking anything, including water. In the Scripture, this type of fast appears to be an exceptional measure in response to a desperate situation. It generally lasted three days.[3] You should undertake this type of fast only if you have clear direction from the Lord and never for more than three days.

A third type of fast is a partial fast or what is sometimes called a Daniel fast. The emphasis here is on limiting the kinds of food that you eat rather than totally abstaining from food. Daniel wrote, "At that time I, Daniel, mourned for three weeks. I ate no choice food; no meat or wine touched my lips; and I used no lotions at all until the three weeks were over."[4] The Bible also mentions a fourth type of fast commonly called a supernatural fast. It is like an absolute fast—where you neither eat nor drink anything including water—except it is longer. It is identified as a supernatural fast because a person cannot survive for more than a few days without water, except through divine intervention. In all of Scripture, there are only two instances of supernatural fasting. In Deuteronomy Moses writes, "When I went up on the mountain to receive the tablets of stone, the tablets of the covenant that the LORD had made with you, I stayed on the mountain forty days and forty nights; I ate no bread and drank no water."[5] The second instance involved Elijah the prophet.[6]

I entered my first extended fast of ten days with high expectations. I turned the television off. I did not read anything other than the Bible and some devotional classics. As far as I was concerned, it was going to be a time when I not only abstained from food, solid or liquid, but also a time when I focused all of my attention toward God. As a result, I anticipated hearing clearly from the Lord. I expected to receive special insight and direction. I expected to feel vibrantly alive to the Lord's nearness, but I did not. All of that came later.

Experience has taught me that the benefits of fasting almost always come after the fast is over. While there may be moments of spiritual revelation during an extended fast, for the most part it is simply hard work. Fasting is not a time of spiritual harvest, nor even a time of planting or plowing. It is more like clearing the land.

The spiritual landscape is covered with stumps, underbrush, and rocks. When you fast you are working with the Spirit to clear the field so it can be plowed and planted. Now that's hard work! Figuratively speaking, you get blisters on your hands, your back hurts, you get sunburned and thirsty, but it's worth it because you are clearing new spiritual territory.

ACTION STEPS:

▼ PRAYERFULLY CONSIDER FASTING ONE DAY EACH WEEK OR AT LEAST ONE MEAL EACH WEEK.

▼ SPEND THE TIME YOU WOULD NORMALLY SPEND EATING IN PRAYER.

▼ BE SENSITIVE TO THE HOLY SPIRIT SHOULD HE CALL YOU TO A LONGER FAST.

THOUGHT FOR THE DAY:

"Neither did Jesus say if you fast (see Matthew 6:16), as though fasting were something the disciples might or might not be led to do or as though it only applied to a select few, apostles or prophets, preachers or leaders. He stated unambiguously, categorically, and without qualification to the mass of His disciples, 'When you fast...' He left us in no doubt that He took it for granted that His disciples would be obeying the leading of the Spirit in this matter of fasting."[7]

Arthur Wallis

SCRIPTURE FOR THE DAY:
"Even now," declares the LORD,
"return to me with all your heart,
with fasting and weeping and mourning."
Rend your heart
and not your garments.
Return to the LORD your God,
for he is gracious and compassionate,
slow to anger and abounding in love,
and he relents from sending calamity.
Joel 2:12-13

✠

PRAYER:

LORD, FASTING IS HARD FOR ME. NOT ONLY DO I CRAVE FOOD, BUT I ALSO HUNGER FOR THE FELLOWSHIP OF MEALTIME—THE CAMARADERIE, THE CONVERSATION. GIVE ME THE STRENGTH TO FAST, TO SATISFY MY DEEPEST BELONGING NEEDS IN RELATIONSHIP WITH YOU. IN YOUR HOLY NAME I PRAY. AMEN.

---

[1] Matthew 6:16-18.
[2] Luke 4:2.
[3] Esther 4:16.
[4] Daniel 10:2-3.
[5] Deuteronomy 9:9.
[6] 1 Kings 19:8.
[7] Arthur Wallis, *God's Chosen Fast* (Fort Washington, PA: Christian Literature Crusade, 1971).

CHAPTER 10

BREAKING SPIRITUAL STRONGHOLDS

For years, ego and ambition held a stronghold in my life, but I was mostly blind to it. What was so obvious to others was invisible to me. Although I realized something was limiting my spiritual growth and effectiveness for God, I had no idea what it was. Little by little, through fasting, God prepared me for the painful truth.

The first critical incident occurred while I was conducting a conference with an evangelist who ministers in the office of a prophet.[1] One night God gave him a vision[2] for me. In this vision I was on a raft with two of my elders. A large green serpent came out of the water and fastened itself onto my leg and began pulling me into the river. The elders attacked it with their oars, but to little avail. The evangelist was watching, helplessly, from the shore. Finally, he left the muddy riverbank only to return almost immediately with a lion, which plunged into the water and attacked the green serpent. They fought furiously, in and out of the water, and the lion finally killed that vile reptile.

When he finished sharing the vision, I asked him what it meant. He said he would rather not tell me. He thought it would be better if the Lord revealed it to me. I'm not really sure why I asked him to interpret it, as I already knew what it meant. The moment he began speaking, it seemed as though a sword pierced my heart. I was in physical pain, so great was the conviction of the Spirit. That green serpent was the spirit of power, and it had fastened itself upon me. It was attempting to destroy me.

Every time I went to prayer for the next six or seven weeks, God revealed another area where I had abused power, where my ego and ambition had caused me to act in unChristlike and hurtful ways. Nor were those painless revelations of insipid facts. No! Each time I literally gasped with pain. I wept in repentance before the Lord. I begged Him to change me, to create a new heart in me, a heart of humility and service.

One day it was the painful memory of a terrible thing I had said to my wife, Brenda, in anger, years before. Although I had apologized, until that moment I had not realized how deeply I had wounded her. There in prayer, in the presence of God, it seemed her pain became mine, and with the pain, a terrible shame. Another day it was a mortal wound I had inflicted to the spirit of a young man named Terry, who was part of the congregation in one of the first churches where I served as pastor. Then there was the day the Lord revealed the hidden depths of my critical spirit, especially toward other ministers. Day after day, week after week, it went on, this terrible soul-searching, this awesome battle between the Lion of the tribe of Judah and that awful serpent called power.

The final breakthrough came during a conference for ministers hosted by our church. As I stepped to the pulpit to lead in prayer, I was suddenly, overwhelmingly, aware of God's presence. Even now, several years later, I can hardly speak of it. Like Isaiah in the temple, I was "undone" on the inside and inwardly I cried, "...Woe is me!...for mine eyes have seen the King, the LORD of hosts."[3] Wave after wave of His glorious love washed over me and as it did, I was overcome with weeping. I could not stand. I fell to my knees and pressed my forehead against the floor. God's overwhelming holiness was all around me and never have I felt so unclean. Every shortcoming, every failure was shamefully obvious, and yet I did not feel condemned. I felt absolutely unworthy. Yet, as paradoxical as it may sound, I also felt totally accepted, completely loved.

Maybe the stronghold of power and ambition in my life could have been broken without the discipline of fasting, but I doubt it. Perhaps I could have experienced that glorious spiritual breakthrough without the discipline of fasting, but I doubt it. There are spiritual strongholds that can be broken no other way, or as Jesus said, "...this kind goeth not out but by prayer and fasting."[4] Suffice it to say that fasting is a key discipline in becoming the man God has called you to be.

There are many other benefits of fasting—increased effectiveness in ministry, anointing for signs and wonders, power in intercessory prayer, spiritual discernment, special guidance, and financial provision to name just a few. Little wonder that John Wesley[5] refused to ordain anyone into the Methodist ministry who did not fast at least twice a week.[6]

ACTION STEPS:

▼ IN PRAYER, ASK THE LORD TO IDENTIFY ANY SPIRITUAL STRONGHOLDS IN YOUR LIFE.

▼ LIST WHATEVER STRONGHOLDS THE LORD HAS REVEALED TO YOU. BE SPECIFIC.

▼ IN PRAYER AND FASTING, ASK THE LORD TO CAST THESE STRONG-HOLDS DOWN AND SET YOU FREE.

THOUGHT FOR THE DAY:

"More than any other single Discipline, fasting reveals the things that control us. This is a wonderful benefit to the true disciple who longs to be transformed into the image of Jesus Christ. We cover up what is inside us with food and other good things, but in fasting these things surface. If pride controls us, it will be revealed almost immediately...Anger, bitterness, jealousy, strife, fear—if they are within us, they will surface during fasting...We can rejoice in this knowledge because we know that healing is available through the power of Christ."[7]

Richard Foster

SCRIPTURE FOR THE DAY:

For though we live in the world, we do not wage war as the world does.
The weapons we fight with are not the weapons of the world.
On the contrary, they have divine power to demolish strongholds.
We demolish arguments and every pretension that sets itself up
against the knowledge of God, and we take captive every
thought to make it obedient to Christ.

2 CORINTHIANS 10:3-5

✠

PRAYER:

LORD, THANK YOU FOR THE DISCIPLINE OF FASTING. THROUGH FASTING AND PRAYER, YOU HAVE GIVEN ME VICTORY OVER THE STRONGHOLDS IN MY LIFE. CONTINUE YOUR HOLY WORK IN ME UNTIL I AM FULLY CONFORMED TO YOUR IMAGE. IN YOUR HOLY NAME I PRAY. AMEN.

[1] See Ephesians 4:11-15.
[2] See Acts 10:1-23.
[3] Isaiah 6:5 KJV.
[4] Matthew 17:21 KJV.
[5] English theologian, evangelist, and founder of Methodism, who lived in the eighteenth century.
[6] Richard Foster, *Celebration of Discipline* (San Francisco, CA: Harper & Row, Publishers, 1978), pp. 44, 45.
[7] Ibid. p. 48.

THE SECOND CHARACTERISTIC OF A MAN OF VALOR IS

COURAGE

"You may never have to face the decision of whether or not to die for your faith, but every day you face the decision of whether or not you will live for it."[1]

DC TALK AND THE VOICE OF THE MARTYRS

CHAPTER 11

GOD'S "WHEELBARROW"

Undoubtedly you are familiar with the story of the high wire artist who announced that he was going to cross Niagara Falls on a tightrope, pushing a wheelbarrow. The scheduled day finally arrived and hundreds of people gathered on both sides of the Falls to witness his daring feat. With bated breath they watched him make his torturous journey, and when he finally reached the safety of the far shore, they roared their approval.

As he prepared for his return trip, he asked the crowd if they believed he could do it again. They responded enthusiastically. To a person they believed he could do it. Raising his hands for silence he asked, "Do you believe I can do it with a person in the wheelbarrow?" With a single voice they shouted, "You can do it!"

Once more he quieted the crowd, and when he had their attention, he asked for a volunteer. A somber silence settled over the crowd, a few whispered among themselves, but no one stepped forward. It was soon apparent that while no one doubted he could do it, neither did anyone trust him enough to get in the wheelbarrow.

When Solomon, one of the wisest men in the Bible, exhorts us to "Trust in the Lord with all [our] heart..." (Proverbs 3:5), he is not talking about the kind of trust that stands in the crowd and cheers. That kind of trust is cheap. The kind of trust he's writing about is courageous. It dares to risk everything, dares to climb in God's "wheelbarrow."

Well do I remember when God asked me to trust Him with my writing career. At the time I had been writing for twelve years and had published two books and scores of articles. Now God was asking me to put my writing on hold in order to concentrate fully on my duties as the senior pastor of Christian Chapel. For the next seven years, I did not write a single thing for publication, and as far as I knew, I might never write again. With a single-minded obedience, I devoted all of my energies to the church.

Yet, it didn't make sense to me. At nineteen, God had called me to write, and it was obvious that He had given me a talent for it. Why, then, would He ask me to give it up? Still, I made a decision to trust the Lord rather than my own understanding. With that decision I found the strength to give up my dream of being an author.

From time to time the itch to write returned, but each time it did, I surrendered it to the Lord once again. After a while I was even able to make peace with my decision. My writing, like the rest of my life, was now in God's hands. In His time I believed He would release me to write again, but if He did not, then I would trust His wisdom.

Imagine my excitement when Honor Books approached me in the spring of 1987. After several meetings and three weeks of prayer (I had to be sure this was God's doing and not just a subtle temptation), I felt released by the Lord to write again. With great joy I returned to my writing, and in the past eighteen years, I have written twenty-five books. Like Solomon I can say, "In everything you do, put God first, and he will direct you and crown your efforts with success."[1]

ACTION STEPS:

▼ EXAMINE YOUR HEART AND LIFE TO SEE IF YOU ARE TRUSTING IN THE LORD WITH ALL OF YOUR HEART. HAVE YOU PLACED YOUR LIFE, YOUR FAMILY, YOUR CAREER, IN GOD'S "WHEELBARROW"?

▼ IF YOU HAVE NOT PUT EVERYTHING IN GOD'S "WHEELBARROW," MAKE A DECISION TO DO SO RIGHT NOW. BE SENSITIVE TO THE THOUGHTS AND IMPRESSIONS THAT COME TO YOU AS YOU WAIT QUIETLY BEFORE THE LORD. NOW BE OBEDIENT TO HIS GUIDANCE, EVEN IF IT ISN'T EASY.

▼ SHARE YOUR DECISION WITH YOUR PASTOR OR A TRUSTED CHRISTIAN FRIEND.

---

[1] dc Talk and The Voice of the Martyrs, *Jesus Freaks* (Tulsa: Albury Publishing, 1999), p. 21.

THOUGHT FOR THE DAY:

"I am afraid of saying 'Yes,' Lord.

Where will You take me?

I am afraid of drawing the long straw,

I am afraid of signing my name to an unread agreement,

I am afraid of the 'yes' that entails other 'yeses.'

"O Lord, I am afraid of Your demands, but who can resist You?

That Your Kingdom may come and not mine,

That Your will may be done and not mine,

Help me to say 'Yes.'"[2]

Michel Quoist

SCRIPTURE FOR THE DAY:

Trust in the LORD with all your heart and lean not on your own understanding; in all your ways acknowledge him, and he will make your paths straight.

PROVERBS 3:5-6

✟

PRAYER:

LORD, TEACH ME TO TRUST YOU WITH THE DAILY EVENTS
OF MY LIFE—THE LITTLE THINGS, THE MUNDANE DETAILS—
THAT I MIGHT HAVE THE COURAGE TO TRUST YOU WITH THE
REALLY IMPORTANT THINGS. IN THE NAME OF JESUS I PRAY. AMEN.

---

[1] Proverbs 3:6 TLB.
[2] Michel Quoist, *Prayers* (Kansas City: Sheed and Ward, 1963), pp. 120, 123.

STEPPING OFF A CLIFF IN THE DARK

Leaving Christian Chapel, where I had served as senior pastor for twelve years, was a moment of truth for me. I had to answer some hard questions. Did I have the courage to turn my back on everything I had worked so hard to attain? Did I have the courage to make a mid-life career change? Did I have the courage to trust the Lord with my future?

Not only would I be giving up the prestige that went with being the senior pastor of a significant church, but I would also be walking away from a very handsome pay package that included an expense account, health insurance, retirement, and paid vacations. I told someone that it was a little like stepping off a cliff in the dark.

Still, the more I thought about it the more convinced I became that this was exactly what God wanted me to do. After weeks of wrestling alone with this decision, I decided to discuss it with my wife, Brenda. When I told her what was on my mind, she surprised me by saying, "What took you so long? I knew it was time for us to leave the pastorate two years ago."

Her response shocked me. I had expected her to try to talk me out of leaving. After all, women are supposed to be concerned about things like security and home. Instead, she urged me to take a chance and follow my heart. She reminded me that as newlyweds we had dreamed of living in a cabin on a lake or in the mountains where I could write. If we were ever going to do it, now was the time.

As appealing as it sounded, I had visions of financial ruin. Although I had written seven books, my royalties amounted to hardly more than grocery money, sometimes less than that. In the previous twelve months, they had totaled a whopping $775. When I reminded Brenda of this, she brushed my concerns aside. "God will provide," she said. "He always has and He always will."

Sixty days later, on August 30, 1992, I officially announced my resignation as the senior pastor of Christian Chapel, effective December 6, 1992. That final Sunday was emotionally wrenching. I managed to make it through the service and the farewell reception without breaking down, but as I was driving away from the church for the last time, the tears came. A flood of bittersweet memories washed over me, and I wondered for just a moment if I had made a terrible mistake.

Although I grieved for months, I never once regretted my decision. Most major life changes are initially experienced as loss followed by a period of grieving that is both normal and appropriate. Grief is a healing emotion providing closure, while regret is an unhealthy fixation on the past. Had I not understood the difference, I might have been thrown for a loop.

The years we spent at Christian Chapel were the most exciting years of our entire lives, but without a doubt, the past twelve years have been the most fulfilling. Not only have Brenda and I been privileged to lead "Forever in Love" marriage seminars and retreats all over the country, but I have also written eighteen books.

With the help of Brenda's parents, we built a small cabin that sits on the side of a mountain overlooking Beaver Lake in northwest Arkansas. Although we live seven miles from the nearest paved road and twenty-five miles from the closest town, we love it. And Brenda was right. God has supplied all of our needs!

Best of all my zest for ministry has returned. I literally love what we are doing. Remember, when you are doing God's work in God's time, it is an investment from which you will get personal returns. You may grow physically weary, but you will not become emotionally depleted "'for [his] yoke is easy and [his] burden is light.'"[1]

ACTION STEPS:

▼ TAKE A FEW MINUTES AND PRAYERFULLY EXAMINE YOUR LIFE. ASK YOURSELF SOME HARD QUESTIONS: 1) *AM I IN THE CENTER OF GOD'S WILL?* 2) *IF NOT, THEN WHY AM I NOT?* 3) *WHAT CHANGES DO I NEED TO MAKE?* BE SPECIFIC.

▼ REVIEW YOUR LIFE AND SEE HOW GOD HAS DIRECTED YOU TO THIS POINT. THANK HIM FOR HIS FAITHFUL PROVISION.

▼ ASK GOD TO GIVE YOU THE COURAGE TO DO EVERYTHING HE IS CALLING YOU TO DO.

THOUGHT FOR THE DAY:

"Give me a hundred men who fear nothing but sin, and desire nothing but God, and I will shake the world. I care not a straw whether they be clergymen or laymen; and such alone will overthrow the kingdom of Satan and build up the Kingdom of God on earth."[2]

John Wesley

SCRIPTURE FOR THE DAY:

"'And now, compelled by the Spirit, I am going to Jerusalem, not knowing what will happen to me there. I only know that in every city the Holy Spirit warns me that prison and hardships are facing me. However, I consider my life worth nothing to me, if only I may finish the race and complete the task the Lord Jesus has given me—the task of testifying to the gospel of God's grace.'"

ACTS 20:22-24

PRAYER:

LORD, THANK YOU FOR GIVING ME THE COURAGE TO FOLLOW THE LEADING OF YOUR SPIRIT, REGARDLESS OF THE RISK. MAY YOUR FAITHFULNESS GIVE ME THE COURAGE TO MAKE WHATEVER CHANGES, TO TAKE WHATEVER RISKS, YOU REQUIRE OF ME IN THE FUTURE. IN YOUR HOLY NAME I PRAY. AMEN.

---

[1] Matthew 11:30.
[2] Paul Lee Tan, *Encyclopedia of 7,700 Illustrations: Signs of the Times* (Chicago: Assurance Publishers, 1979), p. 282.

CHAPTER 13

A MATTER OF
LIFE AND DEATH

Several years ago, I was leading our congregation in a capital funds campaign in preparation for building our new facilities. We called the campaign Operation Faith because we weren't just focusing on money. Rather, we were explaining the vision of the church and challenging our congregation to believe with us. Of course, those who caught the vision were encouraged to give that it might become a reality. For most of us, that meant giving our money, our time, and our talent. For Ben and Rochelle it meant something more—much more. While most of us were trying to decide what God wanted us to give to the capital funds campaign, they were wrestling with far weightier matters. For them it was a matter of life or death.

Ben's sister needed a kidney transplant, and he was a possible donor. From a safe distance that may not seem like such a significant thing, but when it's your kidney, it's an altogether different matter. First, there's the risk of major surgery; then, the lifelong consequences of living with one kidney instead of two, and the increased danger due to illness or injury. What if something happened to that one remaining kidney?

Suddenly it wasn't a theoretical question any more, but a matter of life and death. Ben had to consider his wife and their future children. How would this affect them in the long run? Then there were the "nitty-gritty" things to consider like time off from work without pay, the trip to Minneapolis, loss of vacation time, and the pain of surgery itself.

Ultimately, Ben felt God was asking him to trust Him with his life and his kidney. After much prayer, he concluded that he had no right to live with two kidneys when his sister had none, when she was facing death unless she had a transplant. He could have said let someone else do it, another family member perhaps. He could have encouraged his sister to seek a cadaver kidney. But he didn't. Love wouldn't allow it—his love for her and for God. And so Ben and Rochelle decided that he should donate his kidney, lay down his life, as it were, for his sister.

It wasn't a decision they made lightly, or something they could "undo" once it was done. Their decision had to be made based on a "worse case scenario," on what might happen if Ben were in an accident or contacted a serious illness. Still, having considered all of that and the worst possible consequences, Ben and Rochelle went ahead because that was what they thought God wanted them to do, and it was what they wanted to do too.

A decision like that takes love, and it takes courage! As far as I am concerned, Ben is a real man of valor.

ACTION STEPS:

▼ LET ME CHALLENGE YOU TO SURRENDER YOUR LIFE UNCONDITIONALLY TO THE LORD. MAKE A COMMITMENT TO DO WHATEVER HE ASKS YOU TO DO, NO MATTER HOW GREAT THE RISK.

▼ WHAT IS GOD REQUIRING OF YOU AT THIS MOMENT IN YOUR LIFE? BE SPECIFIC.

▼ WHAT ARE YOU GOING TO DO? BE SPECIFIC.

THOUGHT FOR THE DAY:

"Certainly it is true that behind every human being who cries out for help there may be a million or more equally entitled to attention. But this is the poorest of all reasons for not helping the person whose cries you hear. Where, then, does one begin or stop? How to choose? How to determine which one of a million sounds surrounding you is more deserving than the rest? Do not concern yourself in such speculations. You will never know; you will never need to know. Reach out and take hold of the one who happens to be nearest. If you are never able to help or save another, at least you will have saved one."[1]

Norman Cousins

✟

SCRIPTURE FOR THE DAY:

During harvest time, three of the thirty chief men came down to David at the
cave of Adullam, while a band of Philistines was encamped in the Valley
of Rephaim. At that time David was in the stronghold, and the Philistine
garrison was at Bethlehem. David longed for water and said, "Oh, that
someone would get me a drink of water from the well near the gate of Bethlehem!"
So the three mighty men broke through the Philistine lines, drew water
from the well near the gate of Bethlehem and carried it back to David.
But he refused to drink it; instead, he poured it out before the LORD.
"Far be it from me, O LORD, *to do this!" he said. "Is it not the blood of men*
who went at the risk of their lives?" And David would not drink it.

2 SAMUEL 23:13-17

PRAYER:

LORD, GIVE ME THE COURAGE TO RISK MY LIFE FOR THOSE I LOVE

IF CIRCUMSTANCES SHOULD DEMAND IT. MORE IMPORTANTLY,

GIVE ME THE LOVE AND THE COURAGE TO LAY DOWN

MY LIFE EACH DAY BY CHOOSING THE NEEDS OF OTHERS

OVER MY OWN. IN YOUR HOLY NAME I PRAY. AMEN.

¹ Norman Cousins, *Human Options*, (quoted in *Disciplines for the Inner Life*, by Bob Benson and Michael W.
Benson, Word Books Publisher, Waco, TX, 1985), p. 310.

CHAPTER 14

NOTHING TO FEAR BUT FEAR ITSELF

Imagine being locked in a 9 X 12 foot room in total darkness for months on end. That's what happened to Jim Stovall. He was alive, but he was not living. Every day was the same. He had no way of telling whether it was day or night, for it was always dark. Worst of all, he had no hope of escape.

Depression, cold and bleak, seeped into his spirit. For days at a time he huddled in the darkness, wrapped in despair. Occasionally he roused himself to lash out in frustration, but to no avail. Nothing he did seemed to matter. There was no way out.

Never, not even in his worst nightmares, could he have imagined ending up like that. Being big and strong, he was a natural athlete. In 1980 he was a member of the U.S. Olympic team and a national champion weight lifter. There wasn't anything he couldn't do, no obstacle he couldn't overcome—or so it seemed. How, then, had he ended up a prisoner incarcerated in total darkness?

Was he an international businessman taken hostage by terrorists? Were his captors Muslim extremists intent on torture and mayhem? Was he a prisoner of war incarcerated somewhere in Iraq or Afghanistan, or a Christian missionary in Indonesia or Pakistan being persecuted for his faith?

No. Jim Stovall was a prisoner of his own blindness and fear.

A routine medical exam at age seventeen revealed a hereditary degenerative eye disease. There was no known cure. By the time he graduated from college and entered business, he was legally blind. Still, he refused to let his handicap deter him. For several years he worked as an investment broker for the New York Stock Exchange.

Then one morning he woke up and he could not see. Nothing. Not even his hand in front of his face. He was totally and absolutely blind!

Unable to face life as a blind man, he moved into a 9 X 12 foot room in the back of his Tulsa, Oklahoma, house, fully intending to spend the rest of his life right there.

After months in that room, he asked himself, *What's the worst thing that can happen to me?*

Now, a lot of bad things can happen to a blind guy, and Jim thought of most of them. He could get lost. He could fall down the stairs or trip over the curb. He could get hit by a car, or worst of all, he could embarrass himself. Still, none of them seemed as bad as spending the rest of his life a prisoner of his own fears.

Jim's escape was hardly dramatic. He didn't get up one morning and instantly resume his former life. If the truth be known, he crept out of his 9 X 12 foot cell. With fear and trembling, he stood in the doorway and tried to work up the courage to step across the threshold. It was only fifty feet to the mailbox, but in his mind every step was fraught with danger.

Finally he took the plunge. First one hesitant step, then another. Fumbling and feeling his way down the hallway and across the living room, he made it to the front door. Now he had to leave the safety of his house and venture outside. Gathering his courage, he stepped onto the porch and turned toward the mailbox.

Of all the things Jim Stovall has done—writing books, winning an Emmy award, hosting a talk show, developing the Narrative Television Network—he is most proud of that fifty-foot walk to the mailbox.

"That was huge," he says. "I haven't done anything since that frightened me more.... You realize if that's possible, everything is possible."

ACTION STEPS:

▼ HAVE YOU ALLOWED ANYTHING—THE FEAR OF FAILURE, WHAT OTHERS THINK, SELF-IMPOSED LIMITS, LACK OF EDUCATION—TO LOCK YOU IN A SELF-MADE PRISON?

▼ IF YOU HAVE, IDENTIFY THOSE THINGS THAT ARE KEEPING YOU FROM BECOMING THE MAN GOD HAS CALLED YOU TO BE.

▼ WHAT ARE YOU GOING TO DO ABOUT IT? BE SPECIFIC.

THOUGHT FOR THE DAY:

"Let me assert my firm belief that the only thing we have to fear is fear itself."

Franklin Delano Roosevelt

SCRIPTURE FOR THE DAY:

Have I not commanded you? Be strong and courageous. Do not be terrified; do not be discouraged, for the LORD your God will be with you wherever you go.

JOSHUA 1:9

✠

PRAYER:

LORD, MAKE ME FEARLESS IN MY OBEDIENCE TO YOU. MAY I NEVER BE AFRAID TO DO ANYTHING YOU HAVE CALLED ME TO DO. AND WHEN I AM AFRAID, ENABLE ME TO OVERCOME MY FEAR BY DOING WHAT IS RIGHT NO MATTER THE RISKS. IN THE NAME OF JESUS I PRAY. AMEN.

CHAPTER 15

ARMBANDS AND OTHER ACTS OF COURAGE

For days they have listened to the distant booming of big guns as the sounds of battle draw ever nearer. Now they stand mute or huddle in doorways, as the Nazi war machine rumbles into the capital. Tanks and trucks roar into the Plaza. Troops are deployed. With German efficiency the takeover is completed. The Danish flag is lowered, and in its place the German flag is raised.

In short order the Nazis issue a decree requiring all Jewish people to wear a yellow armband emblazoned with the Star of David, anytime they appear in public. The purpose is to expedite the identification and deportation of the Jews to death camps. Although the law is immoral and unjust, the Danish people are powerless to rescind it.

On the day the law goes into effect, the Danish king appears in public wearing the hated armband. Although he can do nothing to repeal that immoral law, he does the next best thing—he identifies with the Jewish victims. When the Danish people see their king wearing a yellow armband, they quickly follow suit, thus thwarting the Nazi's purpose. In short order it is impossible to distinguish the Jews from the Danes.

Now that is an act of courage, the kind of thing a man of valor would do. Rather than look the other way, while the Nazis rounded up the Jews and sent them to their deaths, the Danish king chose to identify with them. He risked his life, and the life of his people, rather than do nothing.

Men of valor face a similar choice here in America where an immoral law allows children in the womb to be put to death before birth. Since the infamous Roe v. Wade Supreme Court decision in

1973, more than forty-six million unborn children have been "executed" in abortion clinics in the United States.

What, you may be wondering, can you do? You have neither the power to rescind that tragically flawed decision or the authority to put an end to the killing. A sense of powerlessness tempts you to do nothing, but moral outrage demands action—redemptive action.

First, you can educate yourself so you can speak intelligently on the issue. Abortion is not about women's rights, but civil rights, and the child's right to life biblically and morally outweighs the mother's right to choose. Abortion is not a medical treatment, although it is done in a "medical clinic" under that guise. It treats no disease. Its only purpose is to terminate the life of the child in the womb.

Nor are "legal" abortions safe, no matter the rhetoric to that end. According to former abortion clinic operator Carol Everett, "...gross malpractice occurs at many clinics, which the medical establishment usually succeeds in covering up."[1] She goes on to say, "...we were maiming or killing one woman in every 500."[2]

The second thing you can do is, provide viable alternatives for women in a crisis pregnancy. At Christian Chapel we established a crisis pregnancy ministry and an adoption agency. This enabled us to provide housing and medical care for any woman seeking an alternative to abortion. If she chose to give her baby up for adoption, we also helped find a suitable couple to adopt her child.

And finally, you can speak up for those who cannot speak for themselves by identifying with the invisible victims of abortion. For instance, on Sanctity of Life Sunday some years ago, I challenged members of my congregation to wear a red armband on the anniversary of the infamous Roe v. Wade Supreme Court decision legalizing abortion on demand. Virtually every member of my congregation accepted the challenge, and their courageous actions became a prophetic witness in our community.

All over town, the highly visible armbands became an immediate topic of conversation, giving us an opportunity to relate the story of the Danish king and his courageous act. We then explained, "Like the Danish king, we are wearing these red armbands to identify with the

1.5 million innocent children who are put to death before birth each year in the United States. Although we do not have the power to rescind the Supreme Court's immoral and unjust decision, we refuse to look the other way while these little ones are put to death. We are determined to do everything in our power to bring their desperate plight to the attention of those who have the power to do something about it."

The following week one executive told me that wearing that armband was the hardest thing he ever did. He knew his stand would be unpopular with his superiors. Most of his co-workers were openly "pro-choice," and he knew he was risking their ridicule. He could be reprimanded, perhaps even suspended without pay. Still, he dared to do the right thing.

Some may argue that it was an empty gesture, that it changed nothing. In Denmark, they point out, the Jews were still rounded up and shipped to concentration camps to die. In America abortions continue unabated, so why risk it? Because, if we do nothing in the face of crimes against humanity, we will betray ourselves. Sometimes the only person we can save is ourself, and we can only do that by laying down our life for others.

ACTION STEPS:

▼ REMEMBER A TIME WHEN YOU TOOK A PUBLIC STAND, EVEN THOUGH IT MAY NOT HAVE BEEN POPULAR. HOW DID IT MAKE YOU FEEL? DID YOU SUFFER ANY REPERCUSSIONS?

▼ HAS THERE EVER BEEN A TIME WHEN YOU FAILED TO TAKE A STAND WHEN YOU SHOULD HAVE? HOW DID THAT MAKE YOU FEEL?

▼ ASK GOD TO HELP YOU TO ALWAYS DO THE RIGHT THING, THE COURAGEOUS THING, REGARDLESS OF THE COST. NOW BE SENSITIVE AND OPEN TO THE LEADING OF HIS SPIRIT IN THE DAYS AND WEEKS AHEAD.

THOUGHT FOR THE DAY:

"The church has an unconditional obligation to the victims of any ordering of society. There are things for which an uncompromising stand is worthwhile."[3]

Dietrich Bonhoeffer
Hung in Germany for resisting the Nazis 1945

SCRIPTURE FOR THE DAY:

"Do not think that because you are in the king's house you alone of all the Jews will escape. For if you remain silent at this time, relief and deliverance for the Jews will arise from another place, but you and your father's family will perish.
And who knows but that you have come to royal position for such a time as this?"
Then Esther sent this reply to Mordecai: "Go, gather together all the Jews who are in Susa, and fast for me. Do not eat or drink for three days, night or day. I and my maids will fast as you do. When this is done, I will go to the king, even though it is against the law. And if I perish, I perish."

ESTHER 4:13-16

PRAYER:

THANK YOU, LORD, FOR MEN OF VALOR WHO ARE WILLING TO
RISK EVERYTHING TO DO WHAT IS RIGHT. MAKE ME A MAN
LIKE THAT. IN YOUR HOLY NAME I PRAY. AMEN.

---

[1] Don Feder, "Sick of Death," *Pentecostal Evangel*, Nov. 27, 1988, p. 13. Used by permission of Heritage Features Syndicate.
[2] Ibid.
[3] dc Talk and The Voice of the Martyrs, *Jesus Freaks* (Tulsa: Albury Publishing, 1999), p. 199.

CHAPTER 16

THE FEAR OF MEN

It is 1991 and I am in Wichita, Kansas, attending a pro-life rally as part of the "Summer of Mercy." The speaker is dynamic and persuasive. When he finishes, the leaders of Operation Rescue ask for volunteers to risk arrest by nonviolently blocking the entrance to an abortion clinic in a peaceful attempt to prevent mothers from having the child in their wombs put to death.[1]

As the call is issued, my heart begins a slow, heavy beating. Time seems to stand still, and it feels as if I am standing alone in the presence of God. With undeniable clarity I hear Him ask, "Will you go?" It isn't an audible voice, not one I can hear with my ear, but it might as well be. In my spirit I know God is asking me to risk the disapproval of men in obedience to Him. Though I have the utmost respect for the law and those who enforce it, I know there are times when a man must obey God rather than men.[2] Now I find myself face-to-face with fear. I am not so much afraid of being arrested, though I must admit that it is a concern. Nor am I really afraid of the disapproval of my peers and others who might misunderstand what I am doing. No, the thing I fear most is that I might waste my life, might throw it away on a hopeless cause.

In my spirit I am arguing with God, telling Him that I will willingly sacrifice my life if I can be assured that by doing so no more babies will die at the hands of the abortionists. I will gladly exchange my life for the lives of millions of unborn babies. What I am not willing to do is to throw my life away for no good reason. What if I am arrested and spend months, or even years, in jail and nothing changes. That is a risk I simply am not willing to take.

Again God speaks to me, clearly, distinctly, in my spirit. This time He says, "Nothing you do in obedience to Me is ever wasted no matter how it may appear at the time." His words resonate in my spirit—"Nothing you do in obedience to Me is ever wasted..."

Although you may never find yourself trying to decide if you should "rescue" or not, you will be confronted with innumerable opportunities to compromise your faith rather than risk the disapproval of men. In those moments you will have to decide whether you are going to fear and obey God, or man.

In small ways, and sometimes not so small ways, we confront this issue every day in the work place. *Will I compromise my convictions in order to be accepted as one of the guys? Will I look the other way while some unethical things are done in order to close the deal? Will I do the right thing, no matter what the cost, or will I play along rather than risk rocking the boat?*

No one has ever handled this challenge more effectively than Daniel. As a young man, he was taken captive by the Babylonians and transported from his native Jerusalem to Babylon. He was inducted into the service of King Nebuchadnezzar and underwent three years of intense brainwashing—he was taught both the language and the literature of the Babylonians. Furthermore, he was commanded to eat food and wine from the king's table. At this point "...Daniel resolved not to defile himself with the royal food and wine...."[3]

It has been suggested that what "Daniel perceived (correctly) in this food allotment was an effort to seduce him into the lifestyle of a Babylonian through the enjoyment of pleasures he had never before known.... No mention is made of Daniel being confronted with an apology for Babylonian theology or with intellectual arguments against Old Testament faith. The attack was far more subtle than that, and therefore potentially far more lethal. Somebody in Nebuchadnezzar's palace knew enough about the human heart to see that most men have their price, and that good times, comfort, self-esteem, and a position in society are usually a sufficient bid for a soul."[4]

In many ways Daniel's future greatness depended on that single decision. Had he compromised here he would never have found himself in the positions he later occupied, nor would he have been faithful enough to cope with them as he did. "Instead, from the beginning, in what to others seemed a trivial matter, he nailed his colors to the mast. In doing so, he gained a bridgehead into enemy-occupied territory and found himself increasingly strong in the Lord."[5]

It is as true today as it was in Daniel's day: "Fear of man will prove to be a snare, but whoever trusts in the LORD is kept safe."[6]

ACTION STEPS:

▼ CAN YOU THINK OF A TIME WHEN YOU HAD TO CHOOSE BETWEEN PLEASING MEN OR PLEASING GOD? WHAT DID YOU DO? WHY?

▼ HAVE YOU EVER MADE A DECISION BASED ON THE FEAR OF WHAT OTHERS WOULD THINK? PLEASE EXPLAIN. SOLOMON SAYS, "FEAR OF MAN WILL PROVE TO BE A SNARE...." CAN YOU SEE HOW YOUR DECISION TO PLEASE OTHERS HAS LED TO A TRAP? PLEASE EXPLAIN.

▼ RIGHT NOW ASK GOD TO GIVE YOU THE WISDOM AND THE COURAGE TO ALWAYS DO THE RIGHT THING NO MATTER WHAT THE COST.

THOUGHT FOR THE DAY:

"Dietrich Bonhoeffer courageously took a stand to protect Jews against persecution in Nazi Germany, saying, 'Christ wills that the weak and persecuted should be rescued, and He must be obeyed.' Because of this stand, he could no longer support the German state church. He helped create a new group called the 'Confessing Church' and led an 'illegal' seminary. He eventually became active in the resistance movement, which led to his arrest and execution."[7]

Jesus Freaks

SCRIPTURE FOR THE DAY:

Shadrach, Meshach and Abednego replied to the king, "O Nebuchadnezzar, we do not need to defend ourselves before you in this matter. If we are thrown into the blazing furnace, the God we serve is able to save us from it, and he will rescue us from your hand, O king. But even if he does not, we want you to know, O king, that we will not serve your gods or worship the image of gold you have set up."

DANIEL 3:16-18

☧

Prayer:

LORD, GIVE ME THE COURAGE TO DO THE RIGHT THING
NO MATTER HOW MUCH I FEAR THE CONSEQUENCES.
IN THE NAME OF JESUS I PRAY. AMEN.

---

[1] "Civil disobedience" must always be nonviolent. It is never right to resort to acts of violence. We must be careful not to become a "monster" in order to destroy the monster of abortion.

[2] See Acts 4:18-20.

[3] Daniel 1:8.

[4] Sinclair B. Ferguson, *The Communicator's Commentary*, Volume 19: Daniel (Waco: Word, Inc. 1988), pp. 35,36.

[5] Ibid., p. 39.

[6] Proverbs 29:25.

[7] dc Talk and The Voice of the Martyrs, *Jesus Freaks* (Tulsa: Albury Publishing, 1999), p. 159.

CHAPTER 17

HIS ARM OR HIS LIFE[1]

On Saturday, April 26, 2003, Aron Ralston was mountain climbing alone in a remote area of southeastern Utah. While working his way through a narrow opening about three feet wide, he put his right hand on a nearby boulder to brace himself. The huge boulder suddenly shifted, trapping his hand. Try as he might he could neither move the boulder nor wrest his hand free. As darkness fell he knew he was in trouble.

By Tuesday, he was out of water and had pretty much given up hope of being found by other climbers. If he was going to survive, he was going to have to save himself. Having exhausted all hope of freeing his hand, he began to consider the unthinkable—cutting off his arm just below the elbow. Unfortunately the only knife he had was small and the blade was dull. After a halfhearted attempt in which he failed to break the skin, he gave up.

Aron spent most of Wednesday considering exactly what he would have to do to amputate his arm. A tourniquet was a must. He could not afford to lose much blood. After a day and a half without water, he was seriously dehydrated and weak from lack of food. And, according to his best calculations, it was more than a five-mile hike back to his pickup.

Thursday—day five—dawned clear and cool. Steeling his mind for what had to be done, he positioned the tourniquet and picked up his pocketknife. He had no other choice. It was his arm or his life.

Aron's situation reminds me of something Jesus said, "'If your hand or your foot causes you to sin, cut it off and throw it away. It is better for you to enter life maimed or crippled than to have two hands or two feet and be thrown into eternal fire.'"[2]

I've known men trapped just like Aron Ralston—not in some remote canyon in Utah, but in the habits of the flesh. I'm thinking of a Christian musician and songwriter who is addicted to gambling, a minister who is trapped in Internet pornography, and a businessman who has lost everything chasing the "big deal." What do all of these men have in common? Addictive personalities. For them, more is never enough.

Unlike Aron Ralston, they seem blind to their predicament. Death is looking them in the eye and they don't even know it. To their way of thinking they've just made some bad decisions, even taken a wrong turn or two, but it's no big deal. They are not addicted. They can quit anytime they choose.

Does that sound like anyone you know?

When you get in that deep, getting out requires drastic action. For Aron, it was his arm or his life. He couldn't have them both. What will it be for you? Will you cut off every addictive behavior and live, or will you continue in your bondage and die?

Aron was a man of valor and he made the tough choice. After hacking off his arm, he rappelled down a 60-foot cliff and hiked nearly six miles before rescuers spotted him. He was then flown by helicopter to the hospital emergency room where park ranger Steve Swanke told reporters, "I've never seen anybody like him. His will to live is unbelievable. I've been doing this for twenty-five years and I've never seen a warrior like him."

ACTION STEPS:

▼ Prayerfully examine your life. Is there any area where you are in bondage?

▼ If there is, take full responsibility for your addictive behavior. Confess your sins and ask Jesus to set you free.

▼ Now cut off your arm—that is, cut off all contact with those people, places, and things that cause you to sin.

THOUGHT FOR THE DAY:

"There are several factors that determine your vulnerability to temptation. The most obvious, of course, is circumstance. By allowing yourself to be in the wrong place, associating with the wrong people at the wrong time, you make overcoming temptation nearly impossible. You have stacked the deck against yourself!"[3]

Deliver Me

SCRIPTURE FOR THE DAY:

So I find this law at work: When I want to do good, evil is right there with me. For in my inner being I delight in God's law; but I see another law at work in the members of my body, waging war against the law of my mind and making me a prisoner of the law of sin at work within my members. What a wretched man I am! Who will rescue me from this body of death? Thanks be to God—through Jesus Christ our Lord!

ROMANS 7:21-25

✝

PRAYER:

LORD JESUS, DELIVER ME FROM EVIL. GIVE ME THE COURAGE TO CUT OFF ALL CONTACT WITH THOSE THINGS THAT WAR AGAINST MY SOUL, NO MATTER HOW PAINFUL THAT MAY BE. IN YOUR HOLY NAME I PRAY. AMEN.

---

[1] This account was based on information provided by CBS Broadcasting Inc. All Rights Reserved, ©MMIII.
[2] Matthew 18:8.
[3] Richard Exley, *Deliver Me* (Nashville: Thomas Nelson Publishers, 1998), p. 227.

THE THIRD CHARACTERISTIC
OF A MAN OF VALOR IS

LOYALTY

"Our loyalties are important signs of the kinds of persons we have chosen to become. They mark a kind of constancy or steadfastness in our attachments to those other persons, groups, institutions, or ideals with which we have deliberately decided to associate ourselves...loyalty is like courage in that it shows itself most clearly when we are operating under stress. Real loyalty endures inconvenience, withstands temptations, and does not cringe under assault."[1]

WILLIAM J. BENNETT

CHAPTER 18

PUTTING GOD FIRST

Every man has a multiplicity of loyalties. He is loyal to God, to country, to family, to church, to friends, and to his employer. Under ideal circumstances these various loyalties are complimentary. Unfortunately we do not live in an ideal world and events often conspire to bring our loyalties into conflict. Therefore, it is necessary to develop an hierarchy of loyalties to resolve these inevitable conflicts.

The Scriptures teach that our highest loyalty belongs to God and God alone. Deuteronomy 6:5 commands men everywhere to, "Love the LORD your God will all your heart and with all your soul and with all your strength." After God my first allegiance belongs to my family, then to my church, my country, my friends, and my employer.

In the novel *Quo Vadis*, there is a young Roman named Vinicius who is in love with a Christian girl, but because he is a pagan she will not return his love. Without her knowledge he follows her to the secret gathering of the Christians, and there he hears Peter preach. As he listens something happens within him. He becomes convinced that Jesus is the Son of God, and he wants to become His disciple. Yet something holds him back. "He felt that, if he wished to follow that teaching, he would have to place on a burning pile all his thoughts, habits, and character, his whole nature up to that moment, burn them into ashes, and then fill himself with a life altogether different, and an entirely new soul."[2]

Vinicius is right! That's what it means for a man to truly follow Christ. He must renounce all other loyalties, burn them to ashes, and live only for Jesus. "'If anyone would come after me,'" Jesus says, "'he must deny himself and take up his cross and follow me'" (Matthew 16:24).

The early Church understood clearly the call of Christ and the high cost of commitment. This understanding is illustrated in their language. William Barclay says, "...before the end of the first century the word for *witness* and the word for *martyr* had become the same Greek word. The word is *martus;* its original meaning in ordinary Greek is *witness;* but this is the word which came also to mean *martyr,* because in that time the man who was a witness had every chance of being a martyr too."[3]

Thankfully in the United States of America, we have the freedom to practice our faith without risking our lives. The same cannot be said for much of the world. In many countries loyalty to Christ is a crime punishable by death. "It is said that there are more Christian martyrs today than there were in 100 AD—in the days of the Roman Empire. According to a study done at Regent University, there were close to 156,000 Christians martyred around the world in 1998. An estimated 164,00 will be martyred in 1999."[4]

Even if you are never required to lay down your physical life for your loyalty to Christ, you will be required to lay down your way of life. Daily you will have to choose between the way of the world and the will of God, between your self-interests and the cause of Christ. Much anxiety and indecision can be avoided by simply pledging your highest allegiance, your highest loyalty to God. Having done that many of these lesser, daily decisions will take care of themselves.

ACTION STEPS:

▼ IF YOU HAVE NOT MADE AN UNCONDITIONAL SURRENDER TO JESUS CHRIST DO SO NOW. GIVE HIM YOUR HIGHEST LOYALTY.

▼ LIST YOUR PERSONAL HIERARCHY OF LOYALTIES—NOT WHAT YOU THINK THEY SHOULD BE, BUT WHAT THEY ACTUALLY ARE. REMEMBER, YOU CAN OFTEN DETERMINE YOUR LOYALTIES BY THE WAY YOU SPEND YOUR TIME AND YOUR MONEY.

▼ WHAT CHANGES, IF ANY, DO YOU NEED TO MAKE? BE SPECIFIC.

THOUGHT FOR THE DAY:

"Our mission may not involve hanging on a cross, being jailed, or being burned at the stake here in America, but we have other, more invisible obstacles. Ours is a society built by pride, materialism, and dedication to the status quo. In a world built on free will instead of God's will, we must be the Freaks. While we may not be called to martyr our lives, we must martyr our way of life. We must put our selfish ways to death and march to a different beat. Then the world will see Jesus."[5]

Michael Tait

SCRIPTURE FOR THE DAY:

"Do not be afraid of those who kill the body but cannot kill the soul. Rather, be afraid of the One who can destroy both soul and body in hell...Whoever acknowledges me before men, I will also acknowledge him before my Father in heaven. But whoever disowns me before men, I will disown him before my Father in heaven...Anyone who loves his father or mother more than me is not worthy of me; anyone who loves his son or daughter more than me is not worthy of me; and anyone who does not take his cross and follow me is not worthy of me. Whoever finds his life will lose it, and whoever loses his life for my sake will find it."

MATTHEW 10:28,32-33,37-39

☦

PRAYER:

LORD JESUS, I SURRENDER MYSELF TO YOU—ALL THAT I HAVE, ALL THAT I AM, AND ALL THAT I WILL EVER BE. YOUR WISH IS MY COMMAND. MAY YOUR WILL BE DONE IN AND THROUGH ME AS IT IS DONE IN HEAVEN. MAY YOUR KINGDOM COME IN ME AND MAY YOU EVER BE ENTHRONED AS LORD OF MY LIFE. IN YOUR HOLY NAME I PRAY. AMEN.

[1] William J. Bennett, *The Book of Virtues* (New York: Simon & Schuster, 1993), p. 665.
[2] Quoted in William Barclay, *The Beatitudes and the Lord's Prayer for Every Man* (New York and Evanston: Harper and Row, 1963) p. 51.
[3] Ibid., p. 101.
[4] dcTalk and The Voice of the Martyrs, p. 15.
[5] Ibid., p.8.

CHAPTER 19

TURNING BONES
INTO BREAD

Studying the Bible is a little like eating fish—you have to watch out for the bones. But we don't stop eating fish because of a few bones; instead, we lay the bones aside and eat the meat. So it is with the Scriptures. When a difficult passage gets caught in your throat, you don't throw the whole Bible out. Instead, you lay that "bony" passage aside and continue eating the meat of the Word.

On certain occasions, what I first perceived as a bone has turned out to be a choice morsel. Take Exodus 4:24-26, for instance. "At a lodging place on the way, the LORD met Moses and was about to kill him. But Zipporah took a flint knife, cut off her son's foreskin and touched Moses' feet with it. 'Surely you are a bridegroom of blood to me,' she said. So the LORD let him alone. (At that time she said 'bridegroom of blood,' referring to circumcision.)"

The first time I read that passage I almost choked. Like a fish bone, it caught in my throat. It made absolutely no sense to me. In obedience to the Lord's command, Moses was returning to Egypt to confront Pharaoh when God apparently tried to kill him. Several times I just passed over that passage, laid it aside like a bone. Then I began work on a series of biographical sermons on the great personalities of the Bible, beginning with Moses. Once more I was tempted to lay that passage aside, but instead, I decided to read it from at least a half a dozen different translations. The one that quickened my understanding was *The Amplified Bible, Old Testament.* It said, "Along the way at a [resting] place, the Lord met Moses and sought to kill him [made him acutely and almost fatally ill]. [Now apparently he had failed to circumcise one of his sons, his wife being opposed to it; but seeing his life in such danger] Zipporah took a flint knife and cut off the foreskin of her son and cast it to touch Moses' feet, and said, Surely a husband of blood you are to me!"

Suddenly it opened up for me. That inn, that resting place on the way to Egypt, was Moses' Gethsemane. It was his moment of truth. No longer could he please his wife and be loyal to God too. Jehovah demanded circumcision and Zipporah forbid it. The resulting conflict was so severe that Moses became deathly ill. He was a divided man, torn between the wife he loved and the God he served.

As all of us know, our emotions affect our physical bodies. Take anger or fear, for instance. Our heart races, we get short of breath, weak in the knees, and we perspire. Unresolved conflicts tie us in knots. We experience difficulty with digestion, elimination, and sexual performance. Some doctors even advance the theory that there are classic personality types associated with major illnesses. These doctors believe that emotional factors precipitate, or at least are associated with, many diseases.

Such was the case with Moses. He was not deathly ill because there was something organically wrong, nor because God was trying to kill him. The thing that took him to death's door was the internal turmoil created by his desire to please both his God and his wife. God demanded circumcision. Zipporah forbid it. Moses could not please them both, and it was killing him.

Jesus may have had a similar experience in Gethsemane, when He found Himself torn between His Father's will and the desire to save Himself. (See Matthew 26:36-46.) The resulting spiritual agony and inner conflict pushed Him nearly to the point of death. So great was His distress that at one point He sweat great drops of blood. (See Luke 22:44.) Yet, despite His physical symptoms, when He was finally able to pray "'...not my will, but yours be done'" (Luke 22:42), he received strength from above (v. 43) to fulfill His destiny.

Moses experienced his miraculous recovery only when Zipporah finally submitted. Taking a flint knife, she circumcised their son and delivered Moses from his deadly dilemma. Well it has been said, "'No one can serve two masters...'" (Matthew 6:24). The peace God promises comes as a consequence of our loyalty and obedience.

Surrender everything. Give Him your absolute loyalty and His peace will be yours.

ACTION STEPS:

▼ PRAYERFULLY EXAMINE YOUR LIFE TO SEE IF THERE IS ANY AREA WHERE YOUR WILL IS IN CONFLICT WITH GOD'S WILL. IF SO, WHAT ARE YOU GOING TO DO ABOUT IT? BE SPECIFIC.

▼ IS THERE ANY AREA OF YOUR LIFE WHERE THERE IS A CONFLICT BETWEEN GOD'S WILL AND YOUR FAMILY, OR YOUR CAREER? IF SO, WHAT ARE YOU GOING TO DO ABOUT IT? BE SPECIFIC.

▼ CONSIDER DISCUSSING THESE ISSUES WITH YOUR PASTOR OR A TRUSTED BROTHER IN THE LORD.

THOUGHT FOR THE DAY:

"Whether a man arrives or does not arrive at his own destiny— the place that is peculiarly his—depends on whether or not he finds the Kingdom within and hears the call to wholeness—or holiness, as another might say. The man who hears that call is chosen. He does not have to scramble for a place in the scheme of things. He knows that there is a place which is his and that he can live close to the One who will show it to him."[1]

Elizabeth O'Connor

SCRIPTURE FOR THE DAY:

Jesus answered, "If you want to be perfect, go, sell your possessions and give to the poor, and you will have treasure in heaven. Then come, follow me."

MATTHEW 19:21

✟

PRAYER:

LORD JESUS, YOU KNOW HOW MUCH I WANT TO BE LIKED, HOW I CRAVE THE APPROVAL OF OTHERS. DELIVER ME FROM THIS INORDINATE NEED SO I CAN SEEK ONLY YOUR APPROVAL. NOT MY WILL, BUT YOUR WILL BE DONE IN ALL THAT I DO. IN YOUR HOLY NAME I PRAY. AMEN.

---

[1] Elizabeth O'Connor, *Journey Inward, Journey Outward,* quoted in *Disciplines for the Inner Life* by Bob Benson and Michael W. Benson (Waco: Word Books Publisher, 1985), p. 13.

CHAPTER 20

LOYALTY TO GOD, DEATH TO SELF

In Chapter 19, we considered a "bony" passage of Scripture from Exodus 4—"At a lodging place on the way, the LORD met Moses and was about to kill him" (v. 24). Upon careful examination we determined that Moses did almost die, but God was not trying to kill him. His near fatal illness was precipitated by his inner conflicts resulting from his desire to obey God and yet please his wife.

In this chapter, I want us to look at that passage again, from a slightly different perspective. In a certain sense, the Lord did seek to kill Moses—that is, God sought to put to death the "old man" in Moses, his carnal nature. Of this kind of sanctifying experience Paul writes, "For we know that our old self was crucified with him so that the body of sin might be done away with, that we should no longer be slaves to sin."[1]

In many ways I can identify with Moses. Like him, I have resisted the Lord; I have fought hard against the sanctifying work of His Spirit. The greatest fear I had when I considered giving my life completely to Christ was that I would lose my individuality, my uniqueness. To me, the death of self, the crucifixion of the old man, sounded like the end of my identity. I feared—and with some justification considering how many Christians seemed cloned—that I would be turned into some kind of dull, "saintly" personality.

Nothing could have been further from the truth. Surrendering my life fully to Christ freed me to realize my full potential. The abundant life Jesus brings[2] frees us to become all we are destined to be.

To be crucified with Christ means that God puts our self-destructiveness to death. The "old man" is a killer. He is selfish, blindly ambitious, critical, and cruel. He destroys relationships, breaks up marriages, and wrecks homes.

William Temple says, "...there is only one sin, and it is character-istic of the whole world. It is self-will which prefers 'my' way to God's—which puts 'me' in the center where only God is in place. It pervades the universe. It accounts for [all] cruelty...."[3]

I couldn't agree more. Our best intentions are undermined by our pride, by our gluttonous need for recognition and by our insatiable ambition. Left to our own devices we inevitably self-destruct. No wonder Paul writes, "For to be carnally minded is death...."[4]

Take Moses, for instance. Before his sanctifying experience on the way back to Egypt, he was a hot-tempered and violent man. Even his efforts to serve God were short-circuited by his willfulness. But once God broke his stubborn self-will, he went on to become not only Israel's emancipator and lawgiver, but the meekest of all men.[5] Sanctification did not stymie his talents or his personality. To the contrary, it enabled him to realize his full potential by freeing him from the self-destructive power of his carnal nature.

That is not to say that Moses never had to contend with his old nature again, but only that God broke its stranglehold on him. His "old man" still lived, but now he was defeated, leaving Moses free to live in the Spirit.

How, you may be asking, can you experience that kind of libera-tion? How can you escape the tyranny of your destructive self-will? First, come clean with God. Honestly confess those areas where greed and lust control your life. Ask Jesus to break their power, for only He can. Finally, "...count yourselves dead to sin but alive to God in Christ Jesus."[6] You "...count yourselves dead to sin..." by choosing to resist evil, by choosing to do God's will and not your own, by choosing to give Him your absolute allegiance and highest loyalty.

ACTION STEPS:

▼ IDENTIFY ANY "STRONGHOLDS" YOU MAY HAVE IN YOUR LIFE—HABITS OR ATTITUDES THAT ARE STUBBORNLY RESISTANT TO THE REDEMPTIVE WORK OF THE SPIRIT. BE SPECIFIC.

▼ CONSCIOUSLY CHOOSE TO STOP MAKING EXCUSES FOR THESE STRONGHOLDS. CALL THEM WHAT THEY ARE—REBELLIOUS SELF-WILL.

▼ ASK YOUR PASTOR OR A SPIRITUALLY MATURE FRIEND TO JOIN YOU IN PRAYER, ASKING GOD TO BREAK THEIR STRANGLEHOLD ON YOUR LIFE.

THOUGHT FOR THE DAY:

"The golden rule of understanding spiritually is not intellect, but obedience. If a man wants scientific knowledge, intellectual curiosity is his guide; but if he wants insight into what Jesus Christ teaches, he can only get it by obedience. If things are dark to me, then I may be sure there is something I will not do. Intellectual darkness comes through ignorance; spiritual darkness comes because of something I do not intend to obey."[7]

Oswald Chambers

SCRIPTURE FOR THE DAY:

Don't you know that when you offer yourselves to someone to obey him as slaves, you are slaves to the one whom you obey—whether you are slaves to sin, which leads to death, or to obedience, which leads to righteousness? But thanks be to God that, though you used to be slaves to sin, you wholeheartedly obeyed the form of teaching to which you were entrusted. You have been set free from sin and have become slaves to righteousness.

ROMANS 6:16-18

PRAYER:

ALMIGHTY GOD, DEAL WITH ME AS YOU DEALT WITH MOSES. BREAK MY STUBBORN WILL. BE RUTHLESS IN YOUR LOVE AS YOU DEAL WITH MY CARNAL SELF—SHOW NO MERCY TO THE "OLD MAN." CRUCIFY HIM. IN YOUR HOLY NAME I PRAY. AMEN.

[1] Romans 6:6.
[2] John 10:10.
[3] William Temple, *Readings in St John's Gospel* (London: Macmillan, 1963), p. 24.
[4] Romans 8:6 KJV.
[5] Numbers 12:3 KJV.
[6] Romans 6:11.
[7] Oswald Chambers, *My Utmost for His Highest,* quoted in *Disciplines for the Inner Life* by Bob Benson and Michael W. Benson (Waco: Word Books Publisher, 1985), p. 235.

CHAPTER 21

TORN BETWEEN
TWO LOYALTIES

Is there anything worse than being torn between two loyalties? I think not, especially if it means being torn between pleasing God and pleasing your wife. The closet thing to that is the medieval practice of quartering. The victim's ankles and wrists were hitched to four horses that galloped off in opposite directions literally tearing him limb from limb!

That's how Moses must have felt, at the lodging place, on the way back to Egypt.[1] Zipporah, his wife, was there with him but obviously against her will. Undoubtedly she complained every step of the way. I can imagine her saying, "This is senseless," her whining voice grating unmercifully. "How a man of your age could be taken in by such foolishness is beyond me. And what about the boys? Have you no concern for them? What good do you think you can do? Really now, you don't expect to get an audience with Pharaoh do you?"

The issue here was a matter of priorities, loyalties. Moses was committed to God and she was not. He wanted to circumcise their second son, in obedience to God, and she did not. He was determined to deliver the Israelites from bondage. She didn't care if they rotted in Egypt.

Finally Moses could take no more. Torn between obeying God and pleasing his wife, his health broke. For several tense hours, it seemed he would die. Zipporah, no doubt fearful for her husband's life, eventually took a flint knife and circumcised her son, but defiantly. Flinging the bloody foreskin at her husband's feet she hissed, "You are a bloody husband to me," and forty years of marriage fell prey to her hardheadedness. According to Exodus 18:2, Moses sent her and the boys back to Midian, and he went on to Egypt alone.

Centuries later, Jesus discussed the high cost of commitment. "Do not suppose that I have come to bring peace to the earth. I did not come to bring peace, but a sword....a man's enemies will be the members of his own household."[2] "From now on there will be five in one family divided against each other, three against two and two against three. They will be divided, father against son and son against father, mother against daughter and daughter against mother, mother-in-law against daughter-in-law and daughter-in-law against mother-in-law."[3]

Don't be misled. Jesus is not saying that He comes to cause division, but that when one part of the family is fully committed to Him and the others are not, conflict is inevitable.

There are those who would have us believe that if we just become the kind of Christian husband we should be, there wouldn't be any more conflict with our unbelieving spouse. That's not only unrealistic, it's also unscriptural. Granted, proper attitudes can go a long way toward reducing conflicts, and if followed faithfully, can even convert the unbelieving spouse.[4] Still, if the husband is fully committed to Christ and his wife is not, a certain amount of conflict is inevitable.

Faced with the choice of pleasing God or our wife, we must do as Moses did—we must be obedient to God. It will be hard, even painful at times, but it is the only hope for our salvation and the salvation of our family. If Christ and His kingdom are not worthy of our absolute allegiance and our uncompromising obedience, how can we ever expect others to choose Him? Commitment, not compromise, is what brings those we love to Christ. It doesn't work every time—I'll be the first to admit that. But if it doesn't work, nothing else will either.

ACTION STEPS:

▼ PRAYERFULLY EXAMINE YOUR LIFE TO MAKE SURE YOU ARE NOT COMPROMISING YOUR LOYALTY AND OBEDIENCE TO GOD IN ORDER TO PLEASE OTHERS. IF YOU HAVE BEEN, WHAT CHANGES DO YOU NEED TO MAKE? BE SPECIFIC.

▼ PRAYERFULLY EXAMINE YOUR LIFE TO MAKE SURE YOU ARE NOT USING YOUR COMMITMENT TO CHRIST AS A WAY TO BULLY YOUR WIFE AND

FAMILY. IF YOU HAVE BEEN, WHAT CHANGES DO YOU NEED TO MAKE?
BE SPECIFIC.

THOUGHT FOR THE DAY:
"Is my wife more like Christ because she is married to me? Or is she like Christ in spite of me? Has she shrunk from His likeness because of me? Do I sanctify her or hold her back? Is she a better woman because she is married to me? Is she a better friend? A better mother?"[5]

R. Kent Hughes

The secret to winning our families to Christ is total commitment to the Lord, proper attitudes, and faithful patience.

Richard Exley

SCRIPTURE FOR THE DAY:
*"Husbands, in the same way be considerate as you live with your wives,
and treat them with respect as the weaker partner and as heirs with
you of the gracious gift of life, so that nothing will hinder your prayers."*

1 PETER 3:7

PRAYER:
LORD JESUS, GIVE ME THE COURAGE TO BE OBEDIENT TO YOU
NO MATTER WHAT THE COST. YET IN MY FAITHFUL OBEDIENCE
MAKE ME HUMBLE NOT PROUD, GENTLE NOT OVERBEARING,
LOVING NOT MANIPULATIVE. MAY OTHERS SEE YOUR IMAGE IN ME
AND BE DRAWN TO YOU. IN YOUR HOLY NAME I PRAY. AMEN.

---

[1] See Exodus 4:24-26.
[2] Matthew 10:34,36.
[3] Luke 12:52-53.
[4] See 1 Peter 3:1-7.
[5] R. Kent Hughes, *Disciplines of a Godly Man* (Wheaton: Crossway Books, 1991), p. 40.

CHAPTER 22

IN SICKNESS AND
IN HEALTH[1]

When I think of loyalty I think of Dr. Robertson McQuilkin. In March 1990, he announced his resignation as president of Columbia Bible College in order to care for his beloved wife, Muriel, who was suffering from the advanced stages of Alzheimer's disease. In his resignation letter he wrote:

"My dear wife, Muriel, has been in failing mental health for about eight years. So far I have been able to carry both her ever-growing needs and my leadership responsibilities at CBC. But recently it has become apparent that Muriel is contented most of the time she is with me and almost none of the time I am away from her. It is not just 'discontent.' She is filled with fear—even terror—that she has lost me and always goes in search of me when I leave home. Then she may be full of anger when she cannot get to me. So it is clear to me that she needs me now, full-time.

"Perhaps it would help you to understand if I shared with you what I shared at the time of the announcement of my resignation in chapel. The decision was made, in a way, 42 years ago when I promised to care for Muriel 'in sickness and in health...till death do us part.' So, as I told the students and faculty, as a man of my word, integrity has something to do with it. But so does fairness. She has cared for me fully and sacrificially all these years; if I cared for her for the next 40 years I would not be out of debt. Duty, however, can be grim and stoic. But there is more; I love Muriel. She is a delight to me—her childlike dependence and confidence in me, her warm love, occasional flashes of that wit I used to relish so, her happy spirit and tough resilience in the face of her continual distressing frustration. I do not have to care for her, I get to! It is a high honor to care for so wonderful a person."[2]

As a man and a husband, I am deeply moved by Dr. McQuilkin's selfless decision. Intuitively I realize that's the stuff real men are made of—loyalty and commitment. A willingness to stand by our promises when the going gets tough—for better or for worse, in sickness and in health, till death do us part. Yet, I think it would be a mistake to assume that his decision was an isolated choice, independent of the hundreds of lesser choices that went into their forty-two years of marriage. In truth, a decision of that magnitude is almost always the culmination of a lifelong series of smaller, daily decisions. And, as such, it challenges every one of us to examine the choices we make each day and the way we relate to our spouse.

ACTION STEPS:

▼ DETERMINE TO FIND "LITTLE" WAYS TO DAILY LAY DOWN YOUR LIFE FOR YOUR SPOUSE. THINGS LIKE GIVING UP MONDAY NIGHT FOOTBALL TO SPEND THE EVENING WITH HER, OR GIVING UP A SATURDAY GOLF GAME TO GO SHOPPING WITH HER.

▼ EXAMINE ALL OF YOUR RELATIONSHIPS TO MAKE SURE YOU ARE BEING LOYAL TO YOUR WIFE IN ALL YOU DO AND SAY. IF YOU HAVE BEEN DISLOYAL IN WORD OR DEED, CONFESS IT AS SIN AND RECEIVE THE LORD'S FORGIVENESS.

▼ PRAY FOR YOUR WIFE DAILY AND MAKE A COMMITMENT TO ALWAYS SEEK HER HIGHEST GOOD.

THOUGHT FOR THE DAY:

"...nothing is easier than saying words. Nothing is harder than living them, day after day. What you promise today must be renewed and redecided tomorrow and each day that stretches out before you."[3]

Arthur Gordon

SCRIPTURE FOR THE DAY:

"Husbands, love your wives, just as Christ loved the church and gave himself up for her to make her holy, cleansing her by the washing with water through the word, and to present her to himself as a radiant church, without stain or wrinkle or any other blemish, but holy and blameless."

EPHESIANS 5:25-27

✟

PRAYER:

LORD, TEACH ME TO LIVE AND LOVE SELFLESSLY DAY BY DAY SO THAT I WILL BE PREPARED TO LAY DOWN MY LIFE FOR MY WIFE SHOULD THAT DAY EVER COME. IN THE NAME OF JESUS I PRAY. AMEN.

1   Much of this chapter was taken from *Forever in Love* by Richard and Brenda Exley (Tulsa: River Oak, 1997), pp. 213-215.
2   R. Kent Hughes, *Disciplines of a Godly Man* (Wheaton: Crossway Books, 1991), pp. 35,36.
3   R Arthur Gordon, *A Touch of Wonder* (Old Tappan: Fleming H. Revell Company, 1974), p. 20.

CHAPTER 23

LOYALTY EQUALS LOVE
AND DISCIPLINE

As men and fathers, one of our primary responsibilities is the nurture and discipline of our children. Failing here, we face the most painful consequences. Of all our shortcomings, none is more potentially devastating. Even now America is reaping the firstfruits of this bitter harvest. Juvenile violence is increasing at an alarming rate. According to a recent study, one in every five twelfth-graders was injured as a result of violence in school during the past year.[1]

As Chuck Colson points out, "It wasn't so long ago that the weapons of choice among students were rubber bands and spitballs. Today if you check their bags, you're likely to find everything from handguns to knives, razor blades, brass knuckles, and broken beer bottles."[2] No wonder many junior and senior high schools now utilize metal detectors and security guards in an attempt to keep their halls safe.

With our penchant for affixing blame rather than correcting problems, we rush around demanding to know who fouled up. In truth, there is enough blame to go around. The educational system must shoulder its share of the blame for failing in its responsibility to include character education in its curriculum. The Supreme Court bears no little responsibility for issuing a series of decisions that severely undermine school discipline. But no one bears more responsibility than parents. Because we have refused to discipline our children at home, we have made it almost impossible for anyone else to discipline them.

Let me share an incident that is a case in point. My father and I are enjoying the last of our ice cream when a young mother and her two children take the table next to us. They are an attractive family—

she in a glistening white jogging suit and running shoes, the kids in designer jeans and fashionably sloppy pullovers. From all appearances they are a typical yuppie family—young, professional, and politically correct.

Once they are seated, the little guy, who looks to be six or seven years old, thrusts his straw deep into his chocolate shake and sucks hard. With a malevolent gleam in his eye, he withdraws the straw, turns toward his mother and blows. In an instant the front of her white jogging suit is covered with a chocolate mess. I can't bear to watch so I turn my head. I know she is going to "kill" that kid. Imagine my chagrin when I hear her say, "Honey, don't do that."

Honey, don't do that?

What kind of response is that to the willful destructiveness her son has just demonstrated? I risk a glance toward their table only to discover that she is calmly dabbing at the chocolate mess now running down the front of her jacket. Of course, her stern reprimand has properly terrified her mischievous son. Meekly he returns the straw to his shake. Meekly he reloads and meekly he deposits a second load full in his sister's face.

I watch in amazement as his mother calmly leans across the table and begins to wipe chocolate off of her daughter's face. Once more she says, with pseudo sweetness, "Honey, I told you not to do that. Now just look what you've done to Sissy." The kid surveys the damage, gives his mother a satisfied smirk, then turns his attention once more to his shake.

At this point Dad and I make our escape. No telling where that kid is going to turn his straw next. Once in the car we stare at one another dumbly. Finally, I ask, "Did that really happen?" Nodding his head Dad replies, "If you're talking about that little assassin with the straw, it really happened. What that kid needs is a good spanking!"

Apparently that boy's mother is into the philosophy of permissive parenting. Corporal punishment is out, and allowing the child to fully vent his feelings is in—we don't want to thwart his creativity, do we? That may sound good in theory, but real life is an altogether different matter. Already this mother is reaping the consequences of her misguided decisions, and it is only a matter of time until her son trades in his straw for weapons of a more serious kind. In truth, her troubles are just starting. Her dilemma should come as no surprise to those of us familiar with the Scriptures. Proverbs declares, "The rod of correction imparts wisdom, but a child left to himself disgraces his mother."[3]

Contrary to what the psychological gurus say, corporal punishment is not an act of violence, but of discipline. Administered consistently, and balanced with unconditional love, it teaches children respect for God's authority and for the authority of those He has placed over them. When parents refuse to discipline their children for disrespectful and destructive behavior, they teach them to disregard authority and the rights of others.

If you would fulfill your responsibilities as a father, you must commit to the biblical principles of child rearing, including discipline. Biblical discipline is consistent, the rules are clearly defined, and the punishment is appropriate. Discipline must be administered according to the child's behavior, not according to the parent's mood or some other parental whim. Children need to know that every time they are disobedient, they will be punished. This is not cruelty but love, tough love. True biblical discipline is always an expression of love, not anger, and has the child's best interest at heart.

"Discipline without love is tyrannical and produces children who will grow up to be both hostile and afraid. Love without discipline is permissive and trains children to be selfish and obnoxious. But when unconditional love and consistent discipline are combined, they produce children who are emotionally healthy and well-adjusted."[4]

ACTION STEPS:

▼ EXAMINE YOUR PHILOSOPHY OF DISCIPLINE. IS IT BASED ON SCRIPTURE OR ON THE CURRENT PSYCHOLOGICAL MODEL? PLEASE EXPLAIN.

▼ RATE YOURSELF AS A DISCIPLINARIAN USING A SCALE OF ONE TO TEN WITH TEN BEING EXCELLENT. CONSIDER SUCH FACTORS AS CONSISTENCY, FAIRNESS, APPROPRIATENESS, AND LOVE. ASK YOUR WIFE TO RATE YOU AS WELL AND THEN TOGETHER DISCUSS YOUR ANSWERS.

▼ ASK YOURSELF WHAT AREAS, IF ANY, YOU NEED TO IMPROVE IN.
BE SPECIFIC.

THOUGHT FOR THE DAY:

"The Bible offers a consistent foundation on which to build an effective philosophy of parent-child relationships. It is my belief that we have departed from the standard which was clearly outlined in both the Old and New Testaments, and that deviation is costing us a heavy toll in the form of social turmoil. Self-control, human kindness, respect, and peacefulness can again be manifest in America if we will return to this ultimate resource in our homes and schools."[5]

Dr. James Dobson

SCRIPTURES FOR THE DAY:

"He who spares the rod hates his son, but he who loves him is careful to discipline him."

PROVERBS 13:24

"Do not withhold discipline from a child; if you punish him with the rod, he will not die. Punish him with the rod and save his soul from death."

PROVERBS 23:13-14

✝

PRAYER:

LORD, BEING A PARENT ISN'T EASY. I CONSTANTLY FIND MYSELF REACTING INSTEAD OF RESPONDING. I'M TOO BUSY, TOO TIRED, TOO PREOCCUPIED, TOO SOMETHING.... FORGIVE ME, LORD. MY CHILDREN DESERVE BETTER AND THEY NEED MORE. HELP ME TO BECOME THE FATHER THEY NEED, THE ONE YOU HAVE CALLED ME TO BE. IN THE NAME OF JESUS I PRAY. AMEN.

---

[1]   Charles Colson with Nancy R. Pearcey, *A Dance with Deception*, (Dallas: Word Publishing, 1993), p. 41.
[2]   Ibid.
[3]   Proverbs 29:15.
[4]   Richard Exley, *The Making of a Man* (Tulsa: Honor Books, 1993), p. 67.
[5]   James Dobson, *Dr. Dobson Answers Your Questions* (Wheaton: Tyndale House Publishers, Inc., 1982), p. 130.

CHAPTER 24

ONLY ONE LIFE
TO GIVE

Following the September 11, 2001, terrorist attack on the New York City trade center and the Pentagon, Pat Tillman turned down a $3.6 million contract offer from the Arizona Cardinals to join the Army Rangers. Although his family and friends considered his decision an act of unusual courage and sacrifice, he considered it nothing more than his patriotic duty. As Senator John McCain noted, "Tillman viewed his decision as no more patriotic than that of his less fortunate, less renowned countrymen who loved our country enough to volunteer to defend her in a time of peril."

For his decision to choose country over career and duty above self, Pat Tillman paid the ultimate price. On Friday, April 23, 2004, he was killed in a firefight with anti-coalition militia forces about 25 miles southwest of a U.S. military base at Khost, in southeastern Afghanistan. At the time his battalion was involved in Operation Mountain Storm as part of the U.S. campaign against fighters in the al-Qaida terror network and the former Taliban government.

When Dave McGinnis, Tillman's former coach with the Cardinals, learned of his death he said he felt both overwhelming sorrow and tremendous pride. "Pat represented all that was good in sports. He knew his purpose in life. He proudly walked away from a career in football to a greater calling."

In a prepared statement, NFL Commissioner Paul Tagliabue said that Tillman "...personified all the best values of his country and the NFL. He was an achiever and leader on many levels who always put his team, his community, and his country ahead of his personal interests."

As I listened to the country's outpouring of love and appreciation for Pat Tillman's courage and sacrifice, I found myself profoundly moved. Here was a genuine hero, a man's man. While I admire his athletic achievements—as a linebacker at Arizona State University, he was the Pacific 10 Conference's defensive player of the year in 1997. In 2000, he set a Cardinals record with 224 tackles and warmed up for his last training camp by competing in a 70.2-mile triathlon—it is his character traits that I admire most.

As a scholar athlete, he carried a 3.84 grade-point average and graduated with high honors, earning a degree in marketing. He was a loyal teammate who turned down a $9 million, five-year offer sheet from the Super Bowl champions, the St. Louis Rams, in 2001 to remain with the Cardinals. He was a patriotic American who refused to let someone else do it. He is a true man of valor, not because of the way he died in Afghanistan, but because of the way he lived.

ACTION STEPS:

▼ BASED ON THE THINGS YOU KNOW ABOUT PAT TILLMAN MAKE A LIST OF HIS CHARACTERISTICS YOU ADMIRE MOST. WHY DO YOU ADMIRE THESE CHARACTERISTICS?

▼ THINK OF A TIME WHEN YOU CHOSE COUNTRY OVER CAREER OR DUTY OVER SELF. HOW DID IT MAKE YOU FEEL? WHAT HAPPENED AS A RESULT OF YOUR CHOICE? BE SPECIFIC.

THOUGHT FOR THE DAY:

"Americans look to the Revolutionary War to find the two names that mark the extremes of loyalty to country. On one end of the spectrum we find Benedict Arnold, perhaps the most despised name in the nation's history. At the other end stands Nathan Hale. Ever since he was executed by the British on the morning of September 22, 1776, the death of Nathan Hale has been recognized as one of the great moments of American patriotism. But a few persons were around him, yet his characteristic dying words were remembered. He said, 'I only regret, that I have but one life to lose for my country.'"[1]

William J. Bennett

SCRIPTURE FOR THE DAY:

Greater love has no one than this, that he lay down his life for his friends.

JOHN 15:13

✠

PRAYER:

LORD JESUS, I WANT TO BE THE KIND OF MAN WHO
CHOOSES COUNTRY OVER CAREER AND DUTY OVER SELF.
EVEN IF I NEVER HAVE THE OPPORTUNITY TO DO GREAT THINGS,
HELP ME TO DEMONSTRATE GREAT LOYALTY AS I DO ALL THE
LITTLE THINGS THAT MAKE UP MY DAILY LIFE.
IN YOUR HOLY NAME I PRAY. AMEN.

William J. Bennett, *The Book of Virtues* (New York: Simon & Schuster, 1993) pp. 714, 716.

CHAPTER 25

LOYAL FRIENDS

Several years ago, more than thirty now, I was passing through a difficult time in my life. Part of it was my fault, but at the time I couldn't see that. I simply felt betrayed, wounded by the church I had chosen to serve, rejected and misunderstood by my peers. It was a complicated situation, and there is nothing to be gained by delving into the painful details. Suffice it to say that were it not for some special friends I probably would not be in the ministry today.

For a number of months I lived in an ever-deepening depression. I covered it pretty well, but on the inside I felt as though I was dying. I loved God, but I didn't feel like I could trust Him. I loved the ministry, but there didn't seem to be any place for me. I guess I felt betrayed, yet at the same time, I knew there was disobedience in my own heart. In desperation, I turned to some special friends—Bob and Diana Arnold.

Thinking about them, I was almost overwhelmed. They were the first two converts of our ministry in Holly, Colorado. Many a night Bob would call and say, "Diana has just baked a loaf of bread and we've got a bottle of grape juice. Why don't you and Brenda come out and share Communion with us." Suddenly I wanted that, more than anything. I wanted that special relationship, with them, and with Jesus.

Bob and Diana, it turned out, were working on a farm in south-western Kansas. After driving for most of the day and making a half a dozen phone calls, we finally located them. Though they hadn't heard from us in over two years, they were delighted when we showed up. It was as if we had never been apart.

On Saturday I bought a bottle of grape juice, and I asked Diana if she would bake some bread. After we got the kids in bed, we gathered around the scarred coffee table in their living room, just like old times, only now our roles were reversed. Many was the time I had cried and prayed with the two of them, now they wept and prayed with me.

I poured out my heart. I confessed everything—my hurt, my bitterness, even how close I had come to losing my faith. There were a lot of tears then, and a lot of love, and that farmhouse became a holy place, a sanctuary. We broke bread together, celebrated Holy Communion, and this broken man was made whole again.

The circumstances of my life didn't suddenly change. I still didn't have a place to preach or a way of providing for my family, but those things seemed less pressing now, especially in light of the holy thing that had just happened in my life. I was forgiven, I was among friends, I was back home at last, where I belonged. With God, my family, and my friends, I could face anything.

That's the heart of things isn't it?—loyal friends! With them, we can be content whatever the circumstances of our lives. In times of sorrow, they comfort us; in times of weakness, they strengthen us; and in times of success, they celebrate with us. Well it has been said, "A friend loves at all times, and a brother is born for adversity."[1]

ACTION STEPS:

▼ CAN YOU REMEMBER A TIME WHEN A LOYAL FRIEND PROVIDED MUCH NEEDED SUPPORT AND ENCOURAGEMENT? TAKE A FEW MINUTES NOW AND WRITE HIM A NOTE THANKING HIM FOR HIS FRIENDSHIP AND FOR HIS SPECIAL SUPPORT DURING THAT DIFFICULT TIME.

▼ MAKE A LIST OF YOUR SPECIAL FRIENDS, THOSE WHOSE LOYALTY YOU CAN COUNT ON. NOW PRAY FOR THEM ONE BY ONE, BEING SENSITIVE TO ANY THOUGHTS OR IMPRESSIONS YOU MIGHT HAVE WHILE PRAYING.

▼ IF ANY SPECIAL NEEDS OR CONCERNS CAME TO MIND WHILE YOU WERE PRAYING, MAKE A SPECIAL EFFORT TO BE A FRIEND. DO WHAT YOU CAN TO HELP AND ENCOURAGE YOUR FRIEND IN HIS HOUR OF NEED.

THOUGHT FOR THE DAY:

"When I was in a foreign country once, I had to undergo an operation. The days immediately prior to it were extremely painful ones, and my mind and body were considerably worn by the ordeal. I felt terribly alone, entering a hospital in another land to be served by a physician who did not speak my language. On the morning of the day I was to enter the hospital, my wife attended church. She saw there a friend of ours who was a native of the country. 'Tell John,' he said to her, 'that I am holding him in my prayers.' I was standing at the bathroom sink when she told me, combing my hair. The impact of the words, in my nervous condition, was overpowering, and I burst into tears. I felt deliriously happy. To think he was praying for me. Somehow I was no longer alone. I was not far from home; this place was my home; any place would have been my home. I knew that then. I had seen to the heart of things."[2]

John Killinger

SCRIPTURES FOR THE DAY:

"A friend loves at all times, and a brother is born for adversity."

PROVERBS 17:17

While David was at Horesh in the Desert of Ziph, he learned that Saul had come out to take his life. And Saul's son Jonathan went to David at Horesh and helped him find strength in God. 'Don't be afraid,' he said. 'My father Saul will not lay a hand on you. You will be king over Israel, and I will be second to you. Even my father Saul knows this.'"

1 SAMUEL 23:15-17

✠

PRAYER:

LORD, I STARTED TO PRAY, "GIVE ME A FRIEND LIKE THAT."

INSTEAD, I PRAY, "MAKE ME A FRIEND LIKE THAT."

IN THE NAME OF JESUS I PRAY. AMEN.

---

[1] Proverbs 17:17.
[2] John Killinger, *For God's Sake, Be Human* (Waco, TX: Word Book Publishers), p. 149.

THE FOURTH CHARACTERISTIC OF A MAN OF VALOR IS

INTEGRITY

Helmut Thielicke, the great German theologian and pastor who maintained his integrity all through Hitler's Third Reich, said: "The avoidance of one small fib...may be a stronger confession of faith than a whole 'Christian philosophy' championed in lengthy, forceful discussion."[1]

CHAPTER 26

PERSONAL INTEGRITY²

A few weeks ago I was speaking at a men's conference on the subject of personal integrity. In the course of my message, I related a painfully embarrassing incident that occurred while I was on a publicity tour promoting my book titled, *How to Be a Man of Character in a World of Compromise.* The guys listened intently as I told them of arriving late at the airport to discover that I had forgotten to refuel the rental car. That really should not have been a problem since the rental company will gladly refuel the car for about $4.00 a gallon.

Nonetheless, this is where the story takes its most embarrassing turn. When the agent at the check-in counter asked me if I had refueled the car, I lied, or at least I used the "truth" to deceive. Instead of simply answering no, I said, "The fuel gauge is registering full."

Without looking up from her paperwork she asked, "Do you have a receipt for the gasoline?"

Once more I had an opportunity to do the right thing. All I had to do was tell her that I had not refueled the car. Instead, I simply said, "No." She must have sensed I was not being completely truthful because she pressed me. "What," she asked, "was the name of the gasoline station where you refueled the car?"

This time I did not even pretend to tell the truth. "I don't remember," I mumbled as I turned away and walked toward the concourse. I could feel her eyes boring into me, but I didn't look back.

The irony of it all was readily apparent. Even as I was flying around the country promoting a book on character, I was lying through my teeth. If it hadn't been so tragic, it would have been comical. Such duplicity. Such deceit. And for what? Less than ten dollars worth of gasoline. To make matters worse, the money wasn't even coming out of my own pocket. The publisher was covering all of my expenses.

Of course, God dealt with me ever so severely, and I went on to tell the men how I repented of my sin and received His forgiveness. In addition, I informed them I was now dealing with that particular temptation from a position of strength rather than weakness. Now, whenever I rent a car I take the fuel option, which means I pay for a full tank of gas up front, and I can return it completely empty if I choose.

Having bared my soul and confessed my sinfulness before the entire group, I was feeling more than a little vulnerable. It was a risk I had chosen to take in hopes of inspiring other men to take an honest look at themselves. Instead, one man decided to take a closer look at me, or so it seemed at the time. Raising his hand, he asked, "Did you make restitution?"

Stalling for time while I tried to collect my thoughts, I said, "What exactly do you mean by restitution?"

"As I understand restitution," he replied, "it means to right a wrong. I guess what I'm asking is, what did you do to make things right? Did you telephone the attendant at the car rental counter and tell her that you had lied? Did you send a check to the rental company to cover the fuel expense?"

"I wish I could tell you that I did that," I replied. "But the truth is, I did nothing at all. I made no restitution."

In retrospect I don't think the man was trying to embarrass me. In fact, he made it a point to apologize to me after the session. He truly wanted to know what God expects of us when it comes to restitution. What part does it play in personal integrity?

Thinking about it now, I am convinced that integrity requires us not only to confront the damage our sinful choices have produced, but to go a step further. Now we must do everything within our power to right those wrongs, to heal those hurts, and to restore those relationships.

ACTION STEPS:

▼ WHAT IS GOD SAYING TO YOU THROUGH THIS CHAPTER? PAY ATTENTION TO THE THOUGHTS AND FEELINGS YOU ARE EXPERIENCING, FOR THIS IS OFTEN HOW GOD SPEAKS TO US.

▼ WHAT IS GOD ASKING YOU TO DO ABOUT THE ISSUES HE HAS IMPRESSED UPON YOUR HEART AND MIND? BE SPECIFIC.

▼ ARE YOU GOING TO ACT ON HIS PROMPTINGS? WHEN?

THOUGHT FOR THE DAY:

"Integrity is doing the right thing after you have done the wrong thing even when it is the hardest thing."

Pastor Keith Boyer

SCRIPTURE FOR THE DAY:

But Zacchaeus stood up and said to the Lord, "Look, Lord! Here and now I give half of my possessions to the poor, and if I have cheated anybody out of anything, I will pay back four times the amount." Jesus said to him, "Today salvation has come to this house, because this man, too, is a son of Abraham."

LUKE 19:8-9

PRAYER:

LORD JESUS, FORGIVE ME FOR THE TIMES I HAVE SHADED THE TRUTH AND FOR THE TIMES I HAVE USED THE "TRUTH" TO DECEIVE.

HELP ME TO BE A MAN OF INTEGRITY. IN YOUR HOLY NAME I PRAY. AMEN.

---

¹   R. Kent Hughes, *Disciplines of a Godly Man* (Wheaton: Crossway Books, 1991), p. 123.

²   Some of the material in this chapter was first published in *Strength for the Storm* by Richard Exley (Nashville: Thomas Nelson Publishers, 1999), pp. 205, 206.

PERSONAL INTEGRITY
—PART 2[1]—

Noticing the return address on the envelope, I felt my pulse quicken. Although it had been more than twenty years since I had spoken to the sender, I did not need to read the letter to know what it was about. Nonetheless, I extracted the carefully typed pages and began to read. In an instant I was carried back to a distant Sunday evening in 1967.

In my mind I saw it all again. The small sanctuary, furnished with oak pews and deep red carpet. The congregation sitting attentively, made up mostly of blue-collar people whom I had known a good portion of my young life. Our pastor was standing behind the pulpit, the light reflecting off his glasses. He was an unassuming man, almost apologetic in nature. His humility and soft-spoken ways were what initially appealed to the congregation. But, as is often the case, those very characteristics now grated on more than a few of the more influential members.

I had heard the complaints. "He's not a dynamic leader." "His preaching doesn't inspire faith." "I feel worse when I leave church than when I came." "Why does he have to be so melancholy?" On and on it went.

Being young and zealous, I felt it was my responsibility to do something. So on that Sunday night, during testimony time, I stood to my feet and launched into a bombastic testimony about the sufficiency of Christ. Looking straight at our pastor, I concluded, "We must preach our faith, not our doubts. Nobody wants to hear about our doubts. Everybody has enough doubts of their own."

Having delivered the coup de grace I took my seat. Though I had not mentioned Pastor by name, nor referred to him directly in any way, there was no mistaking what I had done. I had rebuked the pastor, the presiding elder in our congregation, and I had done it publicly. Had anyone felt inclined to correct me, since the Scriptures clearly forbid what I had done,[2] I had left myself ample room to protest my innocence. I was merely giving a testimony. Just encouraging the church in the faith.

Meekly I sat with my head bowed humbly as if I were in prayer. Around me I sensed, more than heard, mumurs of approval. After a few seconds I risked a look at our pastor, the man who had given me my start in the ministry. He appeared shell-shocked. His face was a sickly color and filled with hurt. In his eyes I saw what could only be described as a look of betrayal, as if he could not believe what I had done to him.

In a matter of seconds, he seemed to pull himself together and the service went on. Although he did not demand an apology, confrontation not being his style, I knew I owed him one, and a public one at that. During his sermon I sensed the Holy Spirit directing me to make amends, publicly, before the service ended, but I resisted. Finally, the benediction was given and service dismissed.

For two or three days, perhaps as long as a week, I was deeply troubled in my spirit, but in time I was able to put the whole thing behind me. Life went on, and that incident was pushed to the back of my mind, where it joined a number of other "little" things I had chosen to ignore rather than deal with. None of them were very significant, at least from my perspective, but as the years passed, their cumulative weight wore on me. From time to time God would deal with me about one or another of them. So painfully poignant were the memories of my sinful failures in those holy moments that I was often moved to tears. Always I found a wonderful release after acknowledging my sin and receiving God's forgiveness. Yet for all of that I never resolved the incident with my pastor. Occasionally the Holy Spirit would encourage me to apologize, but I always had an excuse. What good would it do after all these years? Surely he had put the incident behind him by now. Nothing good could come from digging it up at this late date.

The letter I now held in my hand was from my former pastor's youngest son. He quickly brought me up to date regarding his parents. He then made reference to the size of the congregation I served, the number of books I had written, and the "success" I had achieved in ministry. Finally, he came to the reason for his letter.

In plain English he described the deep hurt my actions had caused his parents, particularly his father. After reminding me of the investment his father had made in my life and ministry, he asked me if I could find it in my heart to write his father. He made it clear he was not asking me to apologize, just a thank you, perhaps. He concluded by telling me how much it would mean to his father if he could hear from me.

Sitting at my desk I bowed my head and wept. Guilt flooded my soul, and shame. For more than twenty years that good man had lived with the wound I had so thoughtlessly inflicted. He was not bitter, not angry, just hurt.

Would I write him? I would do more than that. I would confess my sin and ask his forgiveness. I would apologize for my reckless words. I would make what restitution I could. Oh thank You Jesus, for giving me one more chance to right that terrible wrong.

As I put pen to paper I felt the weight I had carried all those years slide off my shoulders. Funny how I had never realized how heavy it was until it was gone. When I finally finished writing, the day was nearly done, just a smear of light outside the office window. Kneeling, I asked God to do what I could not do. I asked Him to put His healing hands on Pastor's heart, to heal the deep wounds my careless words had inflicted so many years ago. "Oh God," I prayed, "may my letter of apology have as profound an impact for good as my hurtful words had for evil."

ACTION STEPS:

▼ DO YOU HAVE ANY "LITTLE THINGS" THAT YOU HAVE CHOSEN TO IGNORE? DO YOU HAVE ANY "LITTLE THINGS" THAT YOU NEED TO

APOLOGIZE AND SEEK FORGIVENESS FOR? IF YOU DO, LIST THEM HERE. BE VERY SPECIFIC.

▼ IN PRAYER, ASK GOD HOW BEST TO MAKE AMENDS. IF YOU FEEL UNCLEAR REGARDING A COURSE OF ACTION, SEEK YOUR PASTOR'S COUNSEL OR THAT OF A MATURE CHRISTIAN BROTHER.

▼ NOW HUMBLY ACT ON WHAT THE LORD HAS SHOWN YOU.

THOUGHT FOR THE DAY:

Since much of the collateral damage caused by our sinful choices is of an emotional or spiritual nature, there may be little we can do beyond a heartfelt apology. It should be done humbly, in a way that brings glory to God not attention to ourselves. When apologizing we should be especially sensitive to the feelings of the injured party and his family. Our apology must never cause him or those he loves further pain or embarrassment.

Richard Exley

SCRIPTURE FOR THE DAY:

"Therefore, if you are offering your gift at the altar and there remember that your brother has something against you, leave your gift there in front of the altar. First go and be reconciled to your brother; then come and offer your gift."

MATTHEW 5:23-24

✝

PRAYER:

LORD JESUS, FORGIVE ME FOR I HAVE SINNED AGAINST MY BROTHERS AND SISTERS. I HAVE WOUNDED THEM WITH MY WORDS. HEAL THE WOUNDS I HAVE SO CARELESSLY INFLICTED. RESTORE THEIR DAMAGED SELF-ESTEEM AND MAKE THEM WHOLE. NOW SET A WATCH OVER MY LIPS LEST I SIN AGAIN WITH THE WORDS OF MY MOUTH. IN YOUR HOLY NAME I PRAY. AMEN.

---

[1] Material in this chapter was first published in *Strength for the Storm* by Richard Exley (Nashville: Thomas Nelson Publishers, 1999), pp. 209-212.

[2] See 1 Timothy 5:1.

CHAPTER 28

FINANCIAL INTEGRITY

Larry had two good friends—Walter and Norman. They were unlike each other in every way except for their faith in Jesus Christ. However, even the way they expressed their faith was decidedly different. Walter was actively involved in all the activities of his church; he was highly visible and much loved by everyone. Norman, on the other hand, only attended church on Sunday morning and maintained a low profile. They were both, however, extraordinarily generous givers.

In the course of time, their careers went in opposite directions. Walter made a considerable amount of money in a relatively short time and seemed on the verge of becoming a very wealthy man. Unfortunately, things did not work out, and he eventually lost everything. Norman, according to those who knew him best, seemed to have the proverbial Midas touch—everything he touched turned to gold. He simply went from success to success.

Only God knows for sure why Walter failed in business while Norman prospered, but those who knew them both have made some interesting observations. Most obvious is the way they each viewed money. According to their mutual friend Larry, Walter saw making money as the ultimate goal in business, while Norman considered it merely a consequence—important to be sure, but not the only reason for being in business, not even the most important reason.

There were other differences too. For instance, Norman limited his involvement to ventures he understood. Even then, he was careful to investigate each opportunity fully to make sure there were no surprises. Once he became involved, he developed a detailed plan and followed it through to completion. He was fond of saying, "Never fall in love with the deal."

Walter, on the other hand, fell in love with every deal that came down the pike. He was willing to do business with almost anyone as long as the enterprise was not immoral or illegal. He loved to wheel and deal. The higher the stakes and the greater the risks, the better he liked it. Not infrequently, his deals involved a certain amount of intrigue, and although he was an honest man, the same could not always be said for his partners.

Despite the fact that Walter was an intelligent man, the excitement of the deal seemed to have a way of blinding him to the risks involved. While he acknowledged their existence, in an academic sort of way, he never really comprehended them on an emotional level. They simply were not real to him. As far as he was concerned every deal was a "sure thing." This trait made him a tremendous promoter, and he had an amazing ability to raise venture capital. Unfortunately, it also made him a poor businessman. When he lost his shirt, as it were, a lot of trusting people lost theirs as well.

What is the point in telling you all of this? Just this: Success in business is often nothing more than knowing and heeding the principles of Holy Scripture. Although the Bible is not a textbook on financial matters, it does have a considerable amount to say on the subject. He who manages his business or his personal affairs accordingly will prosper. He who ignores these biblical principles does so to his own harm.

Some of the more fundamental principles include:

1) *A warning against seeking wealth.* "People who want to get rich," according to the apostle Paul, "fall into temptation and a trap and into many foolish and harmful desires that plunge men into ruin and destruction."[1]

2) *A warning against greed.* Jesus said, "...'Watch out! Be on your guard against all kinds of greed....'"[2] Studies show that most bad investments are made out of greed. A man sees an opportunity to get rich quick and it blinds him to the risks involved. Inevitably his family suffers the consequences. As the ancient sage observed, "A greedy man brings trouble to his family...."[3]

3) *A warning against chasing fantasies.* The writer of Proverbs declares: "He who works his land will have abundant food, but he who chases fantasies lacks judgment."[4]

4) *An exhortation to exercise good judgment and seek wise counsel.* If something seems too good to be true, it probably is. "A simple man believes anything, but a prudent man gives thought to his steps."[5] "He

who walks with the wise grows wise, but a companion of fools suffers harm."[6]

5) *An exhortation to be diligent in all you do.* "The plans of the diligent lead to profit as surely as haste leads to poverty."[7]

A wise man makes himself knowledgeable in these matters.

ACTION STEPS:

▼ Examine your personal and/or business practices. Based on your findings make a list of the principles by which you operate.

▼ Make a list of the five biblical principles for financial management and carry it with you in your wallet or on your Palm Pilot. Memorize the accompanying Scriptures.

▼ Examine your personal and/or business practices in light of these principles. What adjustments, if any, do you need to make. Be specific.

THOUGHT FOR THE DAY:

"Be careful who you associate with lest you become entangled with their excesses and be brought down with them.

Choose character above riches and truthfulness above prosperity."

A Private Journal

SCRIPTURE FOR THE DAY:

"Dishonest money dwindles away, but he who gathers money little by little makes it grow."

PROVERBS 13:11

PRAYER:

Lord, help me to be content without being complacent, to be industrious without being greedy, to be prudent without being obsessively cautious. Above all else give me a thankful heart. In the name of Jesus I pray. Amen.

---

[1] 1 Timothy 6:9.
[2] Luke 12:15.
[3] Proverbs 15:27.
[4] Proverbs 12:11.
[5] Proverbs 14:15.
[6] Proverbs 13:20.
[7] Proverbs 21:5.

CHAPTER 29

INTEGRITY IN
THE WORKPLACE

Financial failure is devastating, especially when it involves not only the loss of a business, but the repossession of a person's home and autos as well. In truth, few experiences in life are more humiliating to a man. It strikes at the very core of his being, of his manhood. To him, it is evidence he has failed at his primary responsibility of providing for his wife and children.

Over the years, I've walked through this painful scenario with more than one man. Although each experience is unique, they do have some things in common. In such situations, most men experience a time of depression followed by a period of intense introspection. Those who are able to honestly examine their failure often recover and go on to experience success. On the other hand, those whose introspection is designed only to find a scapegoat usually end up feeling victimized and seem doomed to fail again.

Not infrequently, the root cause is nothing more than poor work habits or outright laziness—what used to be called slothfulness. It manifests itself in a number of different ways. Inattention to details is one. Refusing to do the grunt work that assures success is another. Staying busy without being productive—using busy work to avoid dealing with real issues—is a third. Another common manifestation of slothfulness is the "working lunch," what is commonly referred to as "developing contacts." Finally, there is the "big deal" syndrome. The man caught in this trap is self-deceived. He can't be bothered with making a living or building a business. All of his time and energy is devoted to closing the "big deal," the one that is going to make him an instant millionaire.

"Go to the ant," counsels the ancient sage, "...consider its ways and be wise! It has no commander, no overseer or ruler, yet it stores its provisions in summer and gathers its food at harvest."[1]

From the ant we learn to be self-starters. It doesn't need to be motivated by another; it has no foreman or supervisor. Although it is tiny, and of primitive intelligence, it still has the good sense to work hard and plan ahead. Because it gathers and stores its provisions in the summer, it has plenty when the barrenness of winter comes.

The lazy person, on the other hand, can find a hundred and one excuses for not working. "The sluggard says, 'There is a lion outside!' or, 'I will be murdered in the streets!'"[2] Nor is he open to counsel: "The sluggard is wiser in his own eyes than seven men who answer discreetly."[3]

As a consequence, he is doomed to repeat his mistakes and to suffer repeatedly the accompanying consequences. "I went past the field of the sluggard, past the vineyard of the man who lacks judgment; thorns had come up everywhere, the ground was covered with weeds, and the stone wall was in ruins. I applied my heart to what I observed and learned a lesson from what I saw: A little sleep, a little slumber, a little folding of the hands to rest—and poverty will come on you like a bandit and scarcity like an armed man."[4]

Remember, God will not prosper a lazy person. He blesses the work of our hands, not our idleness. "The sluggard craves and gets nothing, but the desires of the diligent are fully satisfied."[5]

ACTION STEPS:

▼ EXAMINE YOUR WORK HABITS. ARE YOU CONSCIENTIOUS? DO YOU DO MORE THAN IS EXPECTED OF YOU? DO YOU TAKE PRIDE IN YOUR WORK, EVEN THE MUNDANE DETAILS?

▼ IF YOU ARE A DILIGENT AND CONSCIENTIOUS WORKER, SEE IF YOU CAN DETERMINE THE SOURCE OF YOUR WORK ETHIC. DID IT COME FROM YOUR PARENTS, FROM A TEACHER OR A MENTOR, OR FROM SOME OTHER SOURCE?

▼ IF YOU SENSE A NEED FOR IMPROVEMENT IN YOUR JOB PERFORMANCE, SPECIFICALLY LIST THREE OR FOUR CHANGES THAT YOU ARE GOING TO MAKE.

▼ NOW CONSCIOUSLY CHOOSE TO SEE YOUR WORK AS A WORSHIP GIFT THAT YOU DAILY OFFER TO THE LORD.

THOUGHT FOR THE DAY:

"We do not consider manual work as a curse, or a bitter necessity, not even as a means of making a living. We consider it as a high human function. As a basis of human life. The most dignified thing in the life of a human being and which ought to be free, creative. Men ought to be proud of it."[6]

David Ben-Gurion

SCRIPTURE FOR THE DAY:

"Go to the ant, you sluggard; consider its ways and be wise! It has no commander, no overseer or ruler, yet it stores its provisions in summer and gathers its food at harvest. How long will you lie there, you sluggard? When will you get up from your sleep? A little sleep, a little slumber, a little folding of the hands to rest— and poverty will come on you like a bandit and scarcity like an armed man."

PROVERBS 6:6-11

PRAYER:

LORD, I THANK YOU FOR PHYSICAL STRENGTH AND THE ABILITY TO WORK. I THANK YOU FOR USING MY WORK AS A MEANS OF PROVIDING FOR MY WIFE AND CHILDREN. LET MY WORK BE A BLESSING NOT ONLY TO MY EMPLOYER, BUT ALSO TO ALL THOSE WHO BENEFIT FROM WHAT I PRODUCE. BLESS NOW THE WORK OF MY HANDS THIS DAY AND EVERY DAY. IN THE NAME OF JESUS I PRAY. AMEN.

---

[1] Proverbs 6:6-8.
[2] Proverbs 22:13.
[3] Proverbs 26:16.
[4] Proverbs 24:30-34.
[5] Proverbs 13:4.
[6] Tim Hansel, *When I Relax I Feel Guilty* (Elgin: David C. Cook, 1981), p. 34.

CHAPTER 30

INTEGRITY AND CONSTRUCTIVE CRITICISM

Criticism always makes me feel defensive. I handle it better now, but as a young pastor I often became angry and argumentative when criticized. Stubbornly I defended myself, even when I knew I was wrong. Usually, after I had time to calm down, I would come around, but by then it was often too late. Not infrequently, my angry words wounded a fellow believer, and as the wise man notes, "An offended brother is more unyielding than a fortified city...."[1]

Experience taught me to be more discreet. Although I continued to feel attacked, I learned to watch my words. Unfortunately, I could not hide my defensiveness. (Brenda says I am like the octopus who secretes a black, ink-like liquid when it senses danger. Even though I speak softly, and with great politeness, I emit powerful vibes.)

Regardless of what anyone says to the contrary, I continue to find criticism painful. Perhaps that's why it's so hard for me to deal with it. When it is ungrounded, I feel misunderstood and unfairly judged. If it is legitimate, I am grieved because I have not measured up to my own expectations, let alone the expectations of others.

Well do I remember the afternoon two members of the official board of our church met with me to deliver some constructive criticism. They were kind, they did not attack me, but they were also firm in expressing their concerns. As they spoke I experienced an unbearable sadness. My throat got tight, my eyes teared up, and it was all I could do to keep from breaking down. Their concerns were legitimate, the things they were saying were clearly accurate, and I felt like a failure. I'm sure they did not consider me a failure, but in my heart that's how I felt. Although I know I am not the perfect pastor, it always pains me to learn that my shortcomings are obvious to others as well.

We talked at length that afternoon. I sought their advice on ways to address the areas of their concern. After praying together they assured me of their support and once again made themselves available to help in any way they could. All in all it was the most constructive criticism a man could ever hope to receive; still, it was terribly painful.

The Scriptures clearly teach that constructive criticism, painful though it may be, is essential for personal growth and maturity. They declare, "He who ignores discipline despises himself, but whoever heeds correction gains understanding."[2] A man of integrity understands this and disciplines himself to learn from it. With that thought in mind, let me share some of the guidelines I find helpful in evaluating criticism.

1) *Make it a matter of prayer.* There is often an element of truth in even the most malicious criticism. In prayer, ask God if there is anything He is trying to tell you through this criticism. Ask Him to purify your spirit and to ever remind you that He loves the one who may have unjustly criticized you as much as He loves you.

2) *Consider the source.* Although God can use anyone to correct us, He generally speaks through trustworthy people. Therefore, I give considerably more weight to criticism when it comes from a peer or a mature believer.

3) *Carefully weigh the criticism, separating that which is valid from that which is not.* Even the most sincere person is capable of interjecting his personal feelings into a situation; therefore, I am careful not to accept everything carte blanche. On occasion I have found it beneficial to discuss the criticism with a third person in order to get a more objective view.

4) *With God's help make the corrections that are required.* It is seldom easy to admit that we are wrong, especially if it means reversing a decision or changing a public policy, but it is absolutely mandatory. "He who heeds discipline shows the way to life, but whoever ignores correction leads others astray."[3]

ACTION STEPS:

▼ REMEMBER THE LAST TIME YOU WERE CRITICIZED. HOW DID YOU RESPOND? BE SPECIFIC.

▼ USING THE FOUR GUIDELINES LISTED ABOVE REEVALUATE THAT CRITICISM. LIST ANY INSIGHTS OR CONCLUSIONS YOU MIGHT HAVE REACHED. WHAT ACTION, IF ANY, ARE YOU PLANNING TO TAKE?

THOUGHT FOR THE DAY:

"Indeed, this need of individuals to be right is so great that they are willing to sacrifice themselves, their relationships, and even love for it. This need to be right is also one which produces hostility and cruelty, and causes people to say things that shut them off from communication with both God and man."[4]

Ruel Howe

SCRIPTURE FOR THE DAY:

"He who listens to a life-giving rebuke will be at home among the wise. He who ignores discipline despises himself, but whoever heeds correction gains understanding."

PROVERBS 15:31-32

PRAYER:

LORD, MY NEED TO BE RIGHT MAKES IT HARD FOR ME TO ACCEPT CRITICISM. I BECOME DEFENSIVE, JUSTIFY MY BEHAVIOR, OR EVEN FIND FAULT WITH THE ONE WHO SEEKS TO CORRECT ME. FORGIVE ME AND CHANGE ME, I PRAY. GIVE ME A TEACHABLE SPIRIT AND A HUMBLE HEART. MAKE ME TRULY A MAN OF INTEGRITY. IN THE NAME OF JESUS I PRAY. AMEN.

---

1 Proverbs 18:19.
2 Proverbs 15:32.
3 Proverbs 10:17.
4 Ruel Howe, *The Miracle of Dialogue* (Greenwich: The Seabury Press, 1963), p. 93.

CHAPTER 31

INTEGRITY AND MATTERS OF THE HEART

When the Scriptures speak of the heart, they are not referring to the physical organ that circulates blood through the body. Rather, they are referring to the core of an individual's being, who he is as a person. In biblical language, the heart is the source of emotions, the fountainhead of thoughts and desires, the motivating force in life.

All that a man does, whether good or evil, originates in his heart. Jesus said, "A good man out of the good treasure of his heart brings forth good things, and an evil man out of the evil treasure brings forth evil things."[1] Nowhere is this truth more clearly seen than in the life of John Hinkley, Jr.—the man who shot President Ronald Reagan.

In the weeks following his unsuccessful assassination attempt, the bizarre story behind his crime became clear. According to the FBI, Hinkley was acting out a romantic fantasy involving Hollywood actress Jody Foster. His fantasy was a takeoff on the movie *Taxi Driver* in which Foster played a young prostitute pursued by a love-crazed cabby. In a desperate attempt to win her love, the cabby assassinates a government official. Apparently, the deeply disturbed Hinkley thought he could win Foster's love by assassinating the president of the United States.

While the Hinkley case is extreme, to be sure, it is also classic. It graphically demonstrates the connection between a person's secret thoughts, his deepest feelings, and his actions. The implications are clear: Think on something long enough—fantasize about it, feed it— and it will ultimately become overpowering!

While most of us will never fantasize about killing the president of the United States, our secret desires are just as prophetic.

Inevitably, the thoughts and feelings we harbor in our hearts become the attitudes and actions of our lives. Early on, they are just seeds scattered across the soil of our heart. With a minimum of effort we can sweep them away, but if we delay, or worse yet, if we nurture them, they will take root. Even then, we can uproot them; but if we do not act quickly, they will overwhelm us.

Many a man has mistakenly assumed that he could reserve a part of his heart for weeds, only to discover that evil is a malignancy that invades every part of his being. In time its roots reach even into the most sacred areas of his life, choking out all that is good and decent. Ultimately, he finds himself behaving in ways that were once unthinkable to him. To be men of integrity, we must heed the admonition of the wise man when he writes, "Above all else, guard your heart, for it is the wellspring of life."[2]

ACTION STEPS:

▼ TAKE AN INVENTORY OF YOUR HEART. ARE YOU HARBORING ANY UNCLEAN THOUGHTS OR FEELINGS—THINGS LIKE RESENTMENT, JEALOUSY, LUST, OR ANGER?

▼ PRAY PSALM 139:23-24: "SEARCH ME, O GOD, AND KNOW MY HEART; TEST ME AND KNOW MY ANXIOUS THOUGHTS. SEE IF THERE IS ANY OFFENSIVE WAY IN ME, AND LEAD ME IN THE WAY EVERLASTING."

▼ PRAY PSALM 51:10: "CREATE IN ME A PURE HEART, O GOD, AND RENEW A STEADFAST SPIRIT WITHIN ME."

THOUGHT FOR THE DAY:

"Almost every personal defeat begins with our failure to know ourselves, to have a clear view of our capabilities (negative and positive), our propensities, our weak sides."[3]

Gordon MacDonald

"The Bible characters never fell on their weak points but on their strong ones; unguarded strength is double weakness."[4]

Oswald Chambers

SCRIPTURE FOR THE DAY:

"May the words of my mouth and the
meditation of my heart
be pleasing in your sight,
O Lord, my Rock and my Redeemer."

PSALM 19:14

✠

PRAYER:

LORD, CREATE IN ME A CLEAN HEART, A PURE HEART, AND FILL IT
WITH YOUR LOVE AND GOODNESS. HEAL MY WOUNDED SPIRIT AND
DELIVER ME FROM THE OLD HURTS THAT I HAVE SO CAREFULLY KEPT.

FREE ME FROM THE ENVY AND JEALOUSY WHICH HAVE TAKEN
ROOT IN MY SOUL. NOW SET A WATCH OVER MY HEART LEST ANY
UNCLEAN THING TAKE ROOT THERE. IN THE NAME OF JESUS I PRAY. AMEN.

---

[1] Matthew 12:35 NKJV.
[2] Proverbs 4:23.
[3] Gordon MacDonald, *Rebuilding Your Broken World* (Nashville: Oliver-Nelson Books, a division of Thomas Nelson, Inc., Publishers, 1988), p. 30.
[4] Oswald Chambers, *The Place of Help* quoted in *Rebuilding Your Broken World* by Gordon MacDonald (Nashville: Oliver-Nelson Books, a division of Thomas Nelson, Inc., Publishers, 1988), p. 54.

CHAPTER 32

INTEGRITY AND THE CHALLENGES OF SUCCESS

If you really want to know what a man is made of put him under pressure. Let him experience either adversity or success and you will soon discover whether he is a man of integrity or not.

Given a choice, most of us would probably choose to be tested by success even though we realize it is far harder to handle. As Thomas Carlyle, the Scottish essayist and historian, noted, "...for one man who can stand prosperity, there are a hundred who will stand adversity."[1]

Adversity tests a man's character, his ability to hang in there when the going gets tough. Success, on the other hand, tests a man's integrity, his ability to remain true to himself, to remain morally and ethically pure. "When adversity strikes," as Chuck Swindoll points out, "life becomes rather simple. Our need is to survive. But when prosperity occurs, life gets complicated. And our needs are numerous, often extremely complex. Invariably, our integrity is put to the test."[2]

This is what the wise man is talking about when he writes, "The crucible for silver and the furnace for gold, but [a] man is tested by the praise he receives."[3]

Let's consider for a moment what makes success so challenging. First, it tends to produce pride. It tempts a man to believe that he has succeeded through his own efforts and ingenuity, to believe that he is a self-made man.

Nothing could be further from the truth. Every talent and ability any of us has comes from God. We can no more take credit for our gifts than a man seven feet tall can take credit for his height. Nor can we take credit for our success. The Scriptures say, "No one from the east or the west or from the desert can exalt a man. But it is God who judges: He brings one down, he exalts another."[4]

The second thing that makes success so difficult to handle is that it exposes a man to temptations he has never before had to face. Suddenly he has more disposable income than he knows what to do with. He is invited to serve on prestigious boards and committees. Important people seek his advice. He now moves in circles where anything he wants can be had for a price. Powerful people court him, take him into their confidence, put him in their debt. Tragically, many a man discovers that his integrity has not come from a pure heart, but only from lack of an opportunity to do otherwise.

Those who pass the test of praise usually do so because they refuse to take themselves or their achievements too seriously. They see success not as a plum to be picked, but as a responsibility to be fulfilled toward God and their fellow man. Like Daniel of old they are "...neither corrupt nor negligent."[5] And even their enemies are forced to conclude: "...'We will never find any basis for charges against this man....'"[6]

ACTION STEPS:

▼ Both Joseph and Daniel were men of integrity who remained faithful, not only in adversity, but also when they were exalted to positions of great power. Read their stories in Genesis, chapters 37-50, and Daniel, chapters 1-12, and see if you can identify the character traits that enabled them to remain true to their convictions.

▼ Are those same character traits present in your own life? Please explain.

▼ Ask yourself what you can do to prepare yourself for the challenges of success? Be specific.

THOUGHT FOR THE DAY:

"No man can give at once the impressions that he himself is clever and that Christ is mighty to save. If a person does not subdue this craving for attention and recognition, he will fall utterly short of the goal for which he was designed."[7]

James Denney

SCRIPTURE FOR THE DAY:

"The crucible for silver and the furnace for gold,
but man is tested by the praise he receives."

PROVERBS 27:21

✝

PRAYER:

LORD, PREPARE ME FOR WHATEVER THE FUTURE MAY BRING.

GIVE ME THE GIFT OF CONTENTMENT THAT I MIGHT LABOR

IN OBSCURITY IF THAT IS WHAT YOU SHOULD CHOOSE. GIVE ME

GENUINE HUMILITY THAT I MIGHT HANDLE SUCCESS IF THAT IS WHAT

YOU SHOULD CHOOSE. IN THE NAME OF JESUS, I PRAY. AMEN.

[1] John Bartlett, ed., *Familiar Quotations* (Boston: Little, Brown and Company, 1955), p. 475.
[2] Charles R. Swindoll, *Growing Strong in the Seasons of Life* (Portland: Multnomah Press, 1983), p. 356.
[3] Proverbs 27:21.
[4] Psalm 75:6-7.
[5] Daniel 6:4.
[6] Daniel 6:5.
[7] Quoted in *Fatal Conceit* by Richard W. Dortch (Green Forest: New Leaf Press, Inc., 1993), p. 57.

CHAPTER 33

THE REWARDS
OF INTEGRITY

In the competitive world of business where it is every man for himself, where we are told only the most ruthless succeed, it is a great comfort to know God has a plan for our lives. While other men claw and scratch their way to the top, the man of integrity simply rests in the knowledge that "The Lord will fulfill his purpose for me...."[1] That is not to say that he is complacent or lackadaisical for he is not. His work ethic comes from the Scriptures: "Whatever you do, work at it with all your heart, as working for the Lord, not for men."[2]

The difference in the work habits between the man of integrity and the driven man is not so much one of energy or effort, but of motive. The driven man works to get ahead, to advance his career. The man of integrity works to please the Lord. The driven man depends on his own ingenuity to advance his career. The man of integrity trusts the faithfulness of God. He knows if he is faithful over a few things, he will be made ruler over many things.[3]

More than anyone I know, Cliff Taulbert epitomizes this truth. As a black boy growing up in the Mississippi Delta in the 1950s, he knew the harsh reality of racism, but he refused to allow it to make him bitter. After graduating from high school, he boarded the train heading north. Armed with his faith in God and the love of his family, he set out to fulfill his destiny. Little did he know the plans God had for his life.

Following four years in the Air Force, the last two of which were spent serving in the prestigious 89th Presidential Wing, he enrolled at Oral Roberts University in Tulsa, Oklahoma, where he completed his undergraduate studies in business. When the Bank of Oklahoma hired him, he became the first African-American bank officer in the history of Tulsa. While at BOK he completed work on his master's degree from Southwest Graduate School of Banking at Southern Methodist University.

After leaving the Bank of Oklahoma, he founded Freemont Corporation, a diversified marketing and consulting company. Once again the favor of God blessed his efforts, and he experienced a number of significant successes. Among the most notable was the establishment of a worldwide government market for the Stair Master exercise equipment. Also during this time, he became president of Spike Sports Drink, the first Afro-American-owned sports drink company.

During these years Cliff was a part of Christian Chapel, the congregation where I served as senior pastor. Although he was obviously a gifted leader, he had a true servant's heart. For a number of years he served as the head usher at Christian Chapel, a job at which he excelled. He constantly reached out to young men and poured his life into them. Although we shared lunch from time to time, he seldom talked about his business or his dreams. Instead, we talked about the things of the Lord.

For all his success, Cliff never forgot his roots, or the extended family that gave him his identity. He only regretted that his own children would never know the rich heritage that had been his. These voices from the past seemed too significant to simply let pass away, so he began writing a book. *Once Upon a Time When We Were Colored* was originally intended simply to acquaint his children with their family history, but soon its heartwarming appeal made it an international best seller.

It was one of the first foreign books openly provided to Nelson Mandela by the U.S. State Department following his release from prison. It became an interdisciplinary text for high schools across the country and was read in its entirety on National Public Radio. Universities recognized it as a first-person resource for doctoral theses on Southern culture. Invitations for public appearances and speaking engagements poured in. Soon Cliff was traveling and lecturing internationally. For all his success he remained the same Cliff, and most of us at Christian Chapel only heard rumors of the many awards that came his way.

In 1992 he published a sequel titled *Last Train North*. It too had the same heartwarming appeal that made *Once Upon a Time When We Were Colored* so successful. *The Last Train North* won Cliff a Pulitzer Prize nomination as well as a host of other awards. He became the first Afro-American to win the Mississippi Institute of Arts and Letters

Award for nonfiction as the 1993 nonfiction co-winner. He was named 1992 Double Day (First Light) Author and was awarded the 1993 Mississippi Library Association Award.

Cliff's achievements would be significant for any man, but for a black boy born to a gambling man and a high school girl, and who was reared in the Mississippi Delta where racism was a religion, they are nothing short of unbelievable. To Cliff's way of thinking, his success is truly God's doing and as such it should be an inspiration to all of us who are trusting God to fulfill His purposes in our lives.

ACTION STEPS:

▼ MEMORIZE PROVERBS 22:29 AND PSALM 138:7-8. MEDITATE ON THESE VERSES UNTIL THEY BECOME CORE CONVICTIONS IN YOUR LIFE.

▼ DELIBERATELY SURRENDER YOUR LIFE UNCONDITIONALLY TO THE LORD. ASK HIM TO FULFILL HIS PURPOSES IN YOUR LIFE. MAKE THIS A DAILY PRAYER.

THOUGHT FOR THE DAY:

"God has a history of using the insignificant to accomplish the impossible."[4]

Richard Exley

SCRIPTURE FOR THE DAY:

"Do you see a man skilled in his work? He will serve before kings; he will not serve before obscure men."

PROVERBS 22:29

PRAYER:

LORD, SOMETIMES IT IS HARD TO TRUST YOU WITH MY LIFE AND MY CAREER. I AM AFRAID YOUR PLANS FOR ME ARE NOT BIG ENOUGH. FORGIVE ME, LORD, FOR THINKING I KNOW BETTER THAN YOU WHAT IS BEST FOR ME. NOW I PRAY, "NOT MY WILL BUT YOUR WILL BE DONE." IN JESUS' NAME I PRAY. AMEN.

---

[1] Psalm 138:8.
[2] Colossians 3:23.
[3] See Matthew 25:21.
[4] Richard Exley, *The Making of a Man* (1993), p. 186.

CHAPTER 34

MEN OF INTEGRITY

Failure hurts! It's disappointing, embarrassing, humiliating. Say what you will about its benefits—say it builds character, say it teaches us compassion—the fact is, it still hurts. And if you are like most men, when you fail, you are inundated with doubts about your intelligence, your abilities, and your worth. You are embarrassed and tempted to give up. Don't! At least not until you've considered God's record for transforming failures, for turning life's misfits and rejects into dynamic men of integrity!

"When Nathaniel Hawthorne lost his position in the Custom House at Salem, Massachusetts, he came home utterly defeated to tell his wife that he was a complete failure. To his amazement she greeted his dismal news with delight, saying, 'Now you can write your book.' So he sat down and wrote *The Scarlet Letter*, still considered by many critics as the greatest novel ever written in our country."[1]

"Philip Brooks, the noted Episcopal minister who died in the 1890s, had planned to be a teacher and had prepared himself for the profession of teaching. But he failed so ingloriously that he became despondent. Then he prepared himself for the ministry. In this calling he made a huge success."[2]

What am I trying to say? Just this: Failure isn't final. The list of men in the Bible who failed and yet went on to greatness is long and impressive. Joseph was a slave and a prisoner before ascending to power in Egypt. Moses was a murderer and a fugitive before he became the emancipator of the Israelites. David committed adultery, yet we remember him as a man after God's own heart. Peter denied Jesus, yet he became a noted apostle and ultimately died a martyr rather than renounce his Lord. Saul of Tarsus was a zealous persecutor of the Church, yet after his conversion he became the foremost missionary in the early Church and the most prolific writer of the New Testament.

Secular history also has its successful failures, two of the most notable being Abraham Lincoln and Winston Churchill. Both men rose to power in a crisis hour of their nation's history following a string of ignominious failures. And each in his own way became the greatest leader his nation has ever known. As Lincoln lay dying in a little rooming house across from the place where he was shot, a former detractor (Edwin Stanton) said, "There lies the most perfect ruler of men the world has ever seen...[and] now he belongs to the ages."[3]

It is not failure that makes or breaks a man, but how he responds to it. If he can learn from his failures, if he can persist in spite of failure, if he can maintain a positive attitude, a forward look, then he will succeed in life no matter how many times he may fail.

"After a long period of time in which Mr. Edison and his laboratory assistants had performed 699 experiments without finding what they were searching for, one assistant exclaimed in disgust, 'Six hundred and ninety-nine experiments and we have learned nothing.' Mr. Edison replied, 'Oh, yes, we have learned something. We have learned six hundred and ninety-nine things that will not work.' And, according to the report, on their seven hundredth effort they succeeded."[4] "...though a righteous man falls seven times, he rises again...."[5]

ACTION STEPS:

▼ COMPILE YOUR OWN LIST OF SUCCESSFUL "FAILURES"—THAT IS, MEN WHO FAILED BEFORE THEY SUCCEEDED. WHAT CAN YOU LEARN FROM THEM? BE SPECIFIC.

▼ HOW DO YOU RESPOND TO FAILURE IN YOUR OWN LIFE? IT MAY BE HELPFUL TO RECALL A SPECIFIC FAILURE AND TO EXAMINE HOW YOU RESPONDED TO IT.

▼ MAKE A LIST OF THE CHANGES YOU WISH TO MAKE IN THE WAY YOU RESPOND TO FAILURE. BE SPECIFIC.

THOUGHT FOR THE DAY:

"Instead of accepting the fact that no one deserves the right to lead without first persevering through pain and heartache and failure, we resent those intruders. We treat them as enemies, not friends. We forget that the marks of greatness are not delivered in a paper sack by capricious gods. They are not hurriedly stuck onto skin like a tattoo.

"No, those who are really worth following have paid their dues. They have come through the furnace melted, beaten, reshaped, and tempered."[6]

Charles R. Swindoll

SCRIPTURE FOR THE DAY:
"For though a righteous man falls seven times, he rises again, but the wicked are brought down by calamity."
PROVERBS 24:16

PRAYER:

LORD, TEACH ME TO LEARN FROM MY MISTAKES, TO MAKE PEACE WITH MY PAIN, TO SEE FAILURE AS A FRIEND WHO WILL GUIDE ME TO SUCCESS RATHER THAN A FOE TO DESTROY ME. GIVE ME THE COURAGE TO GET UP AND TRY AGAIN, NO MATTER HOW MANY TIMES I FAIL. IN THE NAME OF JESUS I PRAY. AMEN.

[1] Ilion T. Jones, *God's Everlasting Yes* (Waco, TX: Word Books, 1969), p. 24.
[2] Ibid.
[3] Charles R. Swindoll, *Growing Strong in the Seasons of Life* (Portland: Multnomah Press, 1983), p. 69.
[4] Jones, p. 11.
[5] Proverbs 24:16.
[6] Swindoll, p. 70.

THE FIFTH CHARACTERISTIC OF A MAN OF VALOR IS

SEXUAL PURITY

"Men, if we are Christians, it is imperative that we live pure,
godly lives in the midst of our Corinthian, pornotopian
culture. We must live above the horrifying statistics
or the Church will become increasingly irrelevant
and powerless and our children will leave it.
The Church can have no power apart from purity."[1]

CHAPTER 35

FATAL ATTRACTION

Contrary to popular myth, the way to a man's heart is not through his stomach, but through his ego. Let a woman flatter him, make him feel important, indispensable, irresistible, and he will follow her anywhere, even to the doorway of death.

"With persuasive words" the wise man writes, "she led him astray; she seduced him with her smooth talk...he followed her like an ox going to the slaughter...little knowing it will cost him his life."[2]

Once an adulterous relationship begins, it is almost impossible to break it off. Compared to illicit sex, married love can seem dull and uninteresting. It isn't, of course, but in the heat and excitement of an affair, it can seem that way. Extramarital sex confuses excitement (lust) with love, and married sex can never satisfy the unfaithful heart's insatiable desire for illicit excitement. Hence the "fatal attraction."

There are moments of sinful pleasure, to be sure—the excitement of the hunt, the thrill of the conquest—but the end is death.

Death to the adulterer's relationship with God, for his sin has separated him from fellowship with the Lord. Like Adam, after he had partaken of the forbidden fruit, the adulterer ends up dreading God's nearness and looking for someplace where he can hide from His holy love. For a while he may maintain a spiritual facade, he may even fool his friends and family, but at the core of his being he is dead! Where once there burned a holy fire, now there is only ashes.

Death to the adulterer's marriage, for even if he manages to keep the facts of his adultery secret, his very secrecy will rob his marriage of its intimacy, its life. And more likely than not, his adultery will become common knowledge, severely wounding not only his wife, but his children as well.

Adultery also signals the death of the adulterer's self-respect for he has betrayed his own values. Even if no one else ever finds out, he knows. He knows that he is not the faithful husband and godly father he appears to be. He is not the spiritual leader or the man of integrity his friends think he is. As one adulterer so poignantly put it, "It's a terrible thing to know that you are not the man your family and friends think you are."

Yet, as tragic as adultery is, the grace of God is greater still. "...God does not take away life; instead, he devises ways so that a banished person may not remain estranged from him."[3] Through the sacrificial death of Jesus Christ, God has made a way to forgive the adulterer and to reconcile him to Himself.

"'Come now, let us reason together,' says the LORD. 'Though your sins are like scarlet, they shall be as white as snow; though they are red as crimson, they shall be like wool.'"[4]

ACTION STEPS:

▼ EXAMINE YOUR RELATIONSHIPS. IS YOUR MARRIAGE IN GOOD REPAIR? ARE YOU GIVING IT THE TIME AND ATTENTION IT REQUIRES? ARE YOU CURRENTLY INVOLVED IN ANY FRIENDSHIP THAT YOU CANNOT TELL YOUR PASTOR AND YOUR WIFE ABOUT?

▼ IF YOU ARE INVOLVED IN ANY KIND OF INAPPROPRIATE RELATIONSHIP— EVEN IF IT IS NOT YET ADULTERY—CONFESS IT TO THE LORD AND RECEIVE HIS FORGIVENESS. THEN MAKE YOURSELF ACCOUNTABLE TO YOUR PASTOR OR A TRUSTED CHRISTIAN BROTHER.

▼ WITH THE HELP OF YOUR PASTOR OR A CHRISTIAN BROTHER, MAKE A LIST OF GUIDELINES FOR ALL FUTURE RELATIONSHIPS.

THOUGHT FOR THE DAY:

"If we refuse to take the fact of sin into our calculation, refuse to agree that a base impulse runs through men, that there is such a thing as vice and self-seeking, when our hour of darkness strikes, instead of being acquainted with sin and the grief of it, we will compromise straight away...."[5]

Oswald Chambers

SCRIPTURE FOR THE DAY:

"For the lips of an adulteress drip honey, and her speech is smoother than oil;
but in the end she is bitter as gall, sharp as a double-edged sword.
Her feet go down to death; her steps lead straight to the grave."

PROVERBS 5:3-5

PRAYER:

LORD, DON'T LET ME GET AWAY WITH DENYING MY SEXUAL DESIRES
OR WITH PRETENDING THAT I AM NOT TEMPTED. INSTEAD,
TEACH ME TO HONESTLY EVALUATE MY WEAKNESSES AND
TO TAKE APPROPRIATE STEPS TO GUARD MYSELF. REDEEM MY
SEXUAL DESIRES, SANCTIFY THEM, AND MAKE THEM A PURE AND
HOLY GIFT TO MY WIFE. IN THE NAME OF JESUS I PRAY. AMEN.

---

[1] R. Kent Hughes *Disciplines of a Godly Man* (Wheaton: Crossway Books, 1991), p. 30.

[2] Proverbs 7:21-23.

[3] 2 Samuel 14:14.

[4] Isaiah 1:18.

[5] Oswald Chambers, *The Place of Help* quoted in *Rebuilding Your Broken World* by Gordon MacDonald (Nashville: Oliver-Nelson Books, a division of Thomas Nelson, Inc., Publishers, 1988), p. 50.

CHAPTER 36

THE DEADLY DESCENT

If a man fails to take preventative action the first moment sexual temptation whispers its beguiling suggestions, he will nearly always succumb. Not necessarily immediately, but his end is almost always a foregone conclusion. Once the deadly descent toward infidelity begins, it rapidly advances from one stage to the next. Initially he will probably spend significant amounts of time thinking about her, fantasizing about being together. As the "affair" progresses, his fantasies will likely become sexually explicit, though not always. In any case they are deadly, for Jesus said, "...whoever looks at a woman to lust for her has already committed adultery with her in his heart."[1]

The next stage is talking, sharing deeply with one another. Again it starts innocently enough, usually under the pretext of passing along an announcement or an invitation. Then the conversation shifts to more personal things, a favorite book or movie, plans for the future, a childhood experience, or even some personal problem.

During this stage he is careful to assure himself that they are just friends. He may even acknowledge a growing attraction to her, but he has convinced himself that his interest is purely platonic. He is determined to build a friendship not have an affair, or so he tells himself. Unfortunately he is already having an affair—an affair of the heart. Someone other than his wife is satisfying his need for closeness, tenderness, and togetherness.

By now he is deep into rationalization in an attempt to appease his conscience. The Holy Spirit is not fooled and He convicts him, but to no avail. The relationship is too meaningful to give up. She makes him feel special, hangs on every word he says. She understands him in ways no one else ever has.

Next he begins to justify their relationship—carefully cataloging every failure in his marriage. He recounts his wife's shortcomings in deadly detail. He remembers and magnifies every problem they have ever had. She is insensitive and unresponsive. Surely God doesn't expect him to live his entire life in such an unhappy state.

With a little help from such rationalization, their compatibility leads smoothly into tenderness, the tenderness to a need for privacy, the privacy to physical consolation, and the consolation straight to bed.

Once they become sexually intimate, he finds himself caught in a maelstrom of emotions. Guilt and fear haunt him. His self-esteem falters. He lives with the constant fear of being found out. Prayer seems impossible. How can he face God? Yet, even as he writhes in remorse he is driven with excitement and desire. He hates what he is doing, but he feels powerless to stop. He vows to break it off, to go back to just being friends, but to no avail. His good intentions are just that—good intentions—nothing more. Like a moth drawn irresistibly to a flame, he seems destined to self-destruct.

As the affair progresses, his excitement wears off while his guilt and fear increase. Now he feels trapped. There is no way out of the relationship without hurting his lover, yet he can't continue like this indefinitely either. No matter what he does now someone is going to get hurt and hurt bad!

Now he must face the spouse he has betrayed, the children he has disregarded, and the God he has disobeyed. The consequences of his sin will reverberate through eternity, hurting the innocent as certainly as the guilty. The consequences are inevitable:

"Can a man scoop fire into his lap
    without his clothes being burned?
Can a man walk on hot coals
    without his feet being scorched?
So is he who sleeps with another man's wife;
    no one who touches her will go unpunished.
...a man who commits adultery
    lacks judgment;
whoever does so destroys himself."[2]

If you have caught a glimpse of yourself, or your marriage, now is the time to take corrective action. If there is anything dangerous or inappropriate about any relationship in your life, confess it to God and renounce it. Terminate the friendship immediately and make yourself accountable to a trusted Christian friend or to your pastor.

ACTION STEPS:

Study the five early warning signals listed below. Invite the Holy Spirit to examine your heart and your relationships in light of these insights.

1) A GROWING FASCINATION WITH SOMEONE OTHER THAN YOUR SPOUSE. BEWARE WHEN SHE REGULARLY INTRUDES UPON YOUR THOUGHTS, EVEN WHEN YOU ARE WITH YOUR WIFE AND FAMILY.

2) A HEIGHTENED SENSE OF ANTICIPATION WHEN YOU HAVE AN OPPORTUNITY TO BE WITH HER. BEWARE WHEN YOU FIND YOURSELF LOOKING FORWARD TO THOSE OPPORTUNITIES WHEN YOU CAN LEGITIMATELY BE ALONE WITH HER, OR WHEN YOU VOLUNTEER FOR PROJECTS SO THE TWO OF YOU CAN SPEND TIME TOGETHER.

3) A GROWING DESIRE TO CONFIDE IN HER. BEWARE WHEN YOU ARE TEMPTED TO SHARE THE FRUSTRATIONS AND DISAPPOINTMENTS IN YOUR OWN MARRIAGE.

4) AN INCREASED SENSE OF RESPONSIBILITY FOR HER HAPPINESS AND WELL-BEING. BEWARE WHEN YOU THINK MORE ABOUT HER NEEDS THAN THE NEEDS OF YOUR OWN WIFE AND FAMILY.

5) EMOTIONAL DISTANCING FROM YOUR SPOUSE. BEWARE WHEN YOU HAVE AN INCREASING NEED TO KEEP YOUR THOUGHTS AND FEELINGS SECRET FROM YOUR WIFE.

THOUGHT FOR THE DAY:

"Men, put disciplined hedges around your life—especially if you work with women. Refrain from verbal intimacy with women other than your spouse. Do not bare your heart to another woman, or pour forth your troubles to her. Intimacy is a great need in most people's lives—and talking about personal matters, especially one's problems, can fill another's need of intimacy, awakening a desire for more. Many affairs begin in just this way."[3]

R. Kent Hughes

SCRIPTURE FOR THE DAY:

"Another thing you do: You flood the LORD's altar with tears. You weep and wail because he no longer pays attention to your offerings or accepts them with pleasure from your hands. You ask, 'Why?' It is because the LORD is acting as the witness between you and the wife of your youth, because you have broken faith with her, though she is your partner, the wife of your marriage covenant. "Has not the LORD made them one? In flesh and spirit they are his. And why one? Because he was seeking godly offspring. So guard yourself in your spirit, and do not break faith with the wife of your youth."

MALACHI 2:13-15

PRAYER:

LORD, BUILD A HEDGE AROUND OUR MARRIAGE. PROTECT OUR HEARTS FROM THE EVIL ONE. MAKE ME ESPECIALLY SENSITIVE TO THE PROMPTINGS OF THE HOLY SPIRIT, AND MAY I EVER HEED HIS WARNINGS. IN YOUR HOLY NAME I PRAY. AMEN.

---

[1] Matthew 5:28 NKJV.

[2] Proverbs 6:27-29,32.

[3] R. Kent Hughes, *Disciplines of a Godly Man* (Wheaton: Crossway Books, 1991), p. 32.

CHAPTER 37

THE SECRET FRATERNITY

My experience as a pastor and a speaker for numerous men's conferences and retreats has convinced me that pornography is a church-wide problem, affecting ministers and laity alike. I believe I can safely say that more men sin sexually through the use of pornography than in any other way. And it almost always leads to other sexual sins—fornication, adultery, or homosexuality.

How, you may be wondering, can a Christian man become entangled in such a sordid mess? You can be sure it did not happen overnight, nor is it likely that he consciously chose to become a slave to his lust. Most likely it was a chance encounter, a seemingly innocent temptation that he indulged out of curiosity, only to discover that he had given birth to a monster with an insatiable appetite.

One man traces his obsession to an incident that happened when he was fourteen years old. He says, "I was riding my bicycle across an open field on my way home from school when I found a pornographic magazine. That discovery introduced me to masturbation and eventually fornication. The addiction has never left me, not even after I married."

"Shortly after going on the Internet," another confided, "I discovered that porno garbage was everywhere! Out of curiosity I took a peek. What a mistake that was. Within a short time I was addicted, and I couldn't tear myself away. I felt horrible because I could not believe a Christian could have this kind of problem."

Another man, also a Christian, confessed, "Although I struggled with pornography before I gave my life to Jesus Christ, I was not really tempted by it for about two years after my conversion. Then I discovered the Net and somehow I got drawn into it again. I was tempted by how easy it was to view and read pornography without anyone ever knowing. Over the past year, I have almost become addicted to it."

He goes on to say, "I realize it is wrong and feel like the biggest hypocrite, because everyone who knows me considers me a strong Christian."

The power of this kind of sexual temptation is rooted in its secrecy. It flourishes in the dark, behind closed doors, denied and unacknowledged, except for those terrifying times when it exacts its terrible toll. Then it leaves its victim shamed and guilt-ridden, determined that it will never happen again, but still locked in his debilitating silence.

Most Christian men feel that they cannot confess either their sins or their temptations, especially if they are of a sexual nature. And the more respected a man is, the harder it is for him to risk a confession. He has too much to lose; too many people will be hurt. He has a reputation to maintain, an image to protect; only that is all it is—an image. In truth, he is a tormented man, fighting a lonely and losing battle against the sinful habits of a lifetime. He is not a bad man, not a hypocrite. He hates himself for what he has become—a man of God with a secret life.

If the truth were known, he has probably spent many a night in desperate prayer only to succumb again. He really does love the Lord and his wife and children, but he does not know how to find the deliverance he so desperately needs. And if his secret addiction is not overcome, it will destroy him, not immediately perhaps, but eventually. In the end sin will exact its just due.

If you are battling with a secret sexual sin, you know how easy it is to become discouraged. After all, you have prayed and fought this battle for years with only the most limited success. In the depths of despair, following yet another sinful failure, it would be easy to conclude that while God can deliver you from the eternal penalty of sin, He cannot deliver you from its present power. Although your disappointments may far outnumber your victories, you must not allow personal failures to define your theology. They in no way nullify the truth of the Gospel's redemptive power. According to the

Scriptures, the Cross not only provides justification, but redemption and deliverance as well!

The fact of our victory over sin was accomplished when Jesus died on the Cross. It becomes a present reality in our lives as we "...count [ourselves] dead to sin but alive to God in Christ Jesus."[1] In reality, sexual sin can only be defeated by a combination of divine deliverance and daily discipline. Without the direct intervention of the Holy Spirit making the finished work of Christ a present reality in our lives, all attempts at spiritual discipline will be to no avail. On the other hand, deliverance is fleeting at best unless it is lived out day by day. Galatians 5:16 says, "Walk in the Spirit, and you shall not fulfill the lust of the flesh" (NKJV).

ACTION STEPS:

▼ MAKE YOURSELF ACCOUNTABLE TO YOUR PASTOR OR A MATURE CHRISTIAN BROTHER. NO MATTER HOW EMBARRASSING IT IS YOU MUST CONFESS YOUR SECRET SINS.

▼ REMOVE ALL ACCESS TO PORNOGRAPHY FROM YOUR HOME.

▼ AVOID THOSE SITUATIONS—PEOPLE AND PLACES THAT GIVE BIRTH TO TEMPTATION.

▼ DISCIPLINE YOURSELF TO FAST AT LEAST ONE DAY A WEEK IN ORDER TO BREAK THIS STRONGHOLD.

THOUGHT FOR THE DAY:

"He who is alone with his sin, is utterly alone.... The pious fellowship permits no one to be a sinner. So everyone must conceal his sin from himself and from the fellowship. We dare not be sinners.... So we remain alone with our sin, living in lies and hypocrisy. The fact is that we are sinners!"[2]

Dietrich Bonhoeffer

SCRIPTURE FOR THE DAY:

Have mercy on me, O God,
according to your unfailing love;
according to your great compassion
blot out my transgressions.
Wash away all my iniquity
and cleanse me from my sin.
For I know my transgressions,
and my sin is always before me.
Against you, you only, have I sinned
and done what is evil in your sight....
Hide your face from my sins
and blot out all my iniquity.
Create in me a pure heart, O God,
and renew a steadfast spirit within me.
Do not cast me from your presence
or take your Holy Spirit from me.
Restore to me the joy of your salvation,
and grant me a willing spirit, to sustain me.

PSALM 51:1-4,9-12

PRAYER:

LORD JESUS, HAVE MERCY ON ME AND FORGIVE MY SINS.
BUT I NEED MORE THAN FORGIVENESS. I NEED TO BE CHANGED
AND DELIVERED. WRITE YOUR LAWS UPON MY HEART AND
TEACH ME YOUR WAYS SO THAT I MAY NOT SIN AGAINST
YOU OR THOSE I LOVE. IN YOUR HOLY NAME I PRAY. AMEN.

---

[1] Romans 6:11.

[2] Dietrich Bonhoeffer, quoted in Bob Benson and Michael W. Benson, *Disciplines for the Inner Life* (Waco: Word, 1985), pp. 59-60.

CHAPTER 38

MAKE YOURSELF ACCOUNTABLE[1]

Taking a seat in the chair across from me she nervously straightened her skirt, being careful not to make eye contact. After placing her purse on the floor beside her chair, she clasped her hands in her lap and took a deep breath. Obviously she was nervous, and well she might have been for she had come for counseling. Baring one's soul to the pastor is never easy, especially the first time.

While waiting for her to work up the courage to begin, I listened to the noisy silence. My secretary's voice, deadened by the closed door, could be heard over the clatter of a distant printer. The muted noise of traffic from the street below filtered into the stillness, and I gradually became aware of a sexual tension. I was not sure of its source, whether it was coming from her or if it was a product of my own imagination. She had not done anything remotely sexual, nor had I consciously entertained sexual thoughts; nonetheless, the feelings were there.

At last she spoke, and I forced myself to concentrate. With an effort I was able to focus on ministry, but the sexual tension was always present just below the surface—unbidden, unwelcome, but there just the same. Finally the hour was finished, and we closed the session with prayer. After she left I sat at my desk for several minutes trying to make some sense of my feelings. Nothing like this had ever happened to me before, and it left me shaken, frightened.

Walking down the hall I stepped into my associate pastor's office and closed the door. He looked up from his computer screen as I sat down across the desk from him. Without any preamble, I told him what had just transpired and asked him to hold me accountable. Since the lady was scheduled to return for another appointment next week, I asked him to meet with me as soon as her session was over. Looking him in the eye I said, "If I admit that the sexual tension is still present, or if you sense that it is, insist that I refer her to another counselor. If I refuse to do so, please share everything we have talked about with the elder board." He agreed, and we shared a time of prayer before I returned to my office.

As the time for her next appointment approached, I was more than a little nervous. Just before she arrived, I called my associate pastor on the intercom to make sure he remembered our covenant. Of course, he did and I breathed a silent prayer before beginning the session. It was nothing like the first time. There was not even a hint of sexual tension. I was able to concentrate on ministry with no distractions, and we had a productive session.

Following that experience I came to several conclusions, not all of them flattering. Based on the fact that there were absolutely no sexual feelings present during the second session, I could only conclude that the feelings originated with me. I also discovered that what seems so alluring, so mesmerizing, in the secrecy of the imagination is revealed for what it truly is when it is confessed to another. Temptation flourishes in the dark, but it withers and dies when it is brought into the light of accountability.

I tremble when I think of what might have happened had I not had the kind of relationship with my associate pastor that allowed me to share that experience with him. Perhaps I could have conquered those sexual feelings with God's help alone, but given the proliferation of moral failures within the Body of Christ, I did not feel it wise to try. In fact, I am convinced that few believers can consistently overcome temptation without a relationship of this kind with a friend, a spouse, or a pastor.

Relationships of this nature are more than good—they are absolutely essential. They serve several purposes, not the least of which is to provide a safe place where the imprisoning secrets of our hidden life can be disclosed. Freed from our need to pretend, we can finally be about the business of becoming the man we have been called to be.

ACTION STEPS:

▼ IF YOU SUDDENLY FOUND YOURSELF DEALING WITH SEXUAL TEMPTA-TION, WHO WOULD YOU TALK TO ABOUT IT? IF YOU CAN'T THINK OF

ANYONE YOU WOULD FEEL COMFORTABLE DISCUSSING SUCH PRIVATE MATTERS WITH, YOU NEED TO TAKE IMMEDIATE STEPS TO ESTABLISH THAT KIND OF RELATIONSHIP.

▼ ASK SEVERAL OF YOUR CHRISTIAN FRIENDS WHO THEY WOULD GO TO IF THEY WERE DEALING WITH SEXUAL TEMPTATION.

▼ SPEAK WITH YOUR PASTOR OR A CHURCH LEADER ABOUT DEVELOPING AN ACCOUNTABILITY GROUP.

THOUGHT FOR THE DAY:

"Another important step is to confess your temptations and your sin to someone you can trust. Over the years it has been my experience that temptation, which flourishes in secret, somehow loses much of its mesmerizing power when it is confessed and exposed to the light of Christian love. If the Body of Christ is serious about helping one another overcome sexual temptation of all kinds, then we must be about the business of establishing a spiritual support system, in which we can encourage and strengthen one another. It is not likely a person will trust someone enough to share a problem of this magnitude unless he has had opportunity to test the waters by sharing confidences of a less threatening nature."[2]

Richard Exley

SCRIPTURE FOR THE DAY:

Therefore confess your sins to each other and pray for each other so that you may be healed. The prayer of a righteous man is powerful and effective.

JAMES 5:16

PRAYER:

LORD JESUS, THANK YOU FOR GIVING ME FRIENDS AND CO-WORKERS WHO ARE TRUSTWORTHY. THEIR COUNSEL AND SPIRITUAL SUPPORT HAVE BEEN INVALUABLE TO ME AT THE MOST CRITICAL TIMES IN MY LIFE. HELP ME TO BE A FRIEND LIKE THAT. IN YOUR HOLY NAME I PRAY. AMEN.

---

[1] Much of the material for this chapter was originally published in *Deliver Me* by Richard Exley (Nashville: Thomas Nelson Publishers, 1998), pp. 243, 244.

[2] Ibid., pp. 191, 192.

CHAPTER 39

LIVE CIRCUMSPECTLY[1]

There are several factors that determine your vulnerability to sexual temptation. The most obvious, of course, is circumstance. By allowing yourself to be in the wrong place, associating with the wrong people at the wrong time, you make overcoming temptation nearly impossible. You have stacked the deck against yourself!

A second factor is your personality, your temperament. By nature there are certain temptations that appeal to you more than others. For instance, you may be the kind of person who will do almost anything to be accepted—making you especially susceptible to peer pressure. That being the case, choosing the right friends is doubly important if you hope to live an overcoming life.

A third factor is your personal history—those experiences that have shaped and fashioned who you are. Studies indicate that children who come from abusive homes are more likely to grow up to be abusers than those who come from non-abusive families. Similar studies show that women who were victims of incest are more likely to be promiscuous than those who were not. That is not to say that you cannot overcome your past, or the temptations it births, but only that it is a factor that must be worked into the equation. By recognizing the part your past plays in making you vulnerable to certain temptations, you can take whatever steps are necessary to neutralize its power.

If we are serious about overcoming sexual temptation, we will prayerfully examine ourselves, taking into account both our successes and our failures. We will ask the Lord to help us understand why we seem especially susceptible to one temptation and not another; why we are able to resist the offerings of the enemy one time and not the next. This is not morbid introspection but rather the sanctifying work of the Holy Spirit. As the Lord does His deep work—bringing to light our hidden anxieties and the sinful desires we have not even admitted to ourselves—He is in the process of transforming us. Little by little He is conforming us to His very own image.

This is searching prayer, lingering prayer,[2] and it brings to light the hidden things. In His holy presence, we acknowledge our secret sins and receive forgiveness. He lays His healing hands on our wounded spirits, imparting wholeness. Now we are able, not only to concede our sinful desires, but to relinquish them. And as we are more and more fully conformed to His image, we find ourselves ever more resistant to temptation.

Much of what happens in prayer is beneath the surface of our consciousness, but that part which deals with who we are and why we do the things we do is not. With tender mercy the Holy Spirit brings to light our hidden motivations. Little by little we are able to understand how both our personality and our past make us vulnerable to certain temptations. As we prayerfully examine our temptations, we come to see that what we at first assumed to be the enemy's initial thrust was not that at all. Rather, it was the culmination of a series of "little" temptations that led finally to the temptation that did us in. And when we were victorious, we now realize it was because we resisted temptation immediately, rather than giving it a foothold in our lives.

ACTION STEPS:

▼ As painful as it may be, recall a sinful failure. See if you can identify the earliest moment of temptation. It was probably some small thing, seemingly insignificant, hardly noticed.

▼ Now identify the successive steps leading up to the sinful act itself. Repeat the process with two or three other failures and see if you can identify a pattern.

▼ If you are repeatedly tempted in the same areas (i.e., lust, anger, greed, or some addictive behavior), examine your daily life and habits to see what behaviors make you susceptible to these temptations.

▼ ASK THE LORD TO HELP YOU MAKE WHATEVER ADJUSTMENTS ARE
NECESSARY IN YOUR LIFESTYLE IN ORDER TO WALK IN VICTORY.

THOUGHT FOR THE DAY:

"—Read no books and see no pictures which inflame desire. If the
book you have innocently purchased is doing that, lay it aside; if a
picture is the offender, get up and leave the place.

"—Indulge in no stories nor listen to any that have an unclean sex-
reference. Turn away from the company where these are the vogue.

"—Avoid anything which lowers your inhibitions. How does the
use of alcoholic beverages appear in the light of such a test?

"—Set a watch at the door of your eyes. Lusting often begins
with looking.

"Guard your imagination. In a contest between the will and imagination, the imagination usually wins. Your will is unlikely to be able
to cope with an imagination full of impure imagery. 'Whatsoever
things are pure'—let these fill your imagination.

"—Do not run into temptation. Some associations are very
corrupting.

"—Restrain your indulgent curiosity. That is especially important
for youth. 'The fruit of the tree of knowledge of good and evil' has
cost more than one youth his Eden.

"—Let your thoughts dwell on what to do and be rather than on
what to avoid or shun.

"Especially keep your mind occupied with Christ and the pattern
He has given you."[3]

Albert E. Day

SCRIPTURE FOR THE DAY:

My son, pay attention to what I say;
listen closely to my words.
Do not let them out of your sight,
keep them within your heart;
for they are life to those who find them
and health to a man's whole body.
Above all else, guard your heart,
for it is the wellspring of life.
Put away perversity from your mouth;
keep corrupt talk far from your lips.
Let your eyes look straight ahead,
fix your gaze directly before you.
Make level paths for your feet
and take only ways that are firm.
Do not swerve to the right or the left;
keep your foot from evil.

PROVERBS 4:20-27

PRAYER:

LORD JESUS, HELP ME TO RECOGNIZE TEMPTATION THE FIRST MOMENT
IT APPROACHES ME. HELP ME TO RESIST IT IMMEDIATELY AND
NOT DELAY. MAY I FIND MY STRENGTH AND MY PURITY IN YOU
AND IN YOUR WORD. IN YOUR HOLY NAME I PRAY. AMEN.

---

[1] Much of the material in this chapter was first published in *Deliver Me* by Richard Exley (Nashville: Thomas Nelson Publishers, 1998), pp. 227-229.

[2] See Psalm 139:23-24.

[3] Albert E. Day, *Discipline and Discovery,* quoted in *Disciplines for the Inner Life* by Bob Benson and Michael W. Benson (Waco: Word Books Publisher, 1985), pp. 264, 265.

CHAPTER 40

COUNT THE COST

I hung up the telephone in a daze. A spiritual leader in our congregation had just been arrested for soliciting a prostitute who turned out to be an undercover police officer. I was shocked—there must be some mistake. I was angry—how could he do this to his wife and children, to his church, to me? I was deeply disappointed; I was grieved in my spirit.

And I was afraid. For months the national news had been filled with the tragic details of moral failure at the highest levels of both the Church and the government. As bad as that was, this was somehow worse. Those who had fallen were household names, to be sure, but this struck closer to home. Fearfully, I found myself wondering where it would end, wondering if anyone was safe from the enemy's snares.

Like a siren in the night, that tragic telephone call set off an alarm in my spirit. I could no longer pretend that it was only "bad" men who committed sexual sins. Evidence to the contrary was simply too compelling. Reluctantly, I concluded that a man cannot live in our sexually satiated society and long escape sexual temptation. Instead, he must prepare for it, he must be equipped to overcome it.

As I prayed and searched the Scriptures, the Lord revealed some principles which, if adhered to, will enable a man to overcome sexual temptation.

Principle #1: *Listen to the counsel of godly men.* "My son, keep my words and store up my commands within you...they will keep you from the adulteress, from the wayward wife with her seductive words."[1]

Principle #2: *Make a covenant with your eyes.* On the eve of his wedding, one young man asked me how he could be sure that he would never find a woman he desired more than his wife. My advice to him was simple: "Stop looking!"

Let Job be your example. He, "...made a covenant with [his] eyes not to look lustfully at a girl."[2] The man who is serious about avoiding sexual sin will not window shop. He will have eyes only for his wife.

Principle #3: *Guard your thought life.* Most sexual sin begins in the imagination. Temptation comes first as a thought, then it becomes a desire. *The Living Bible* says, "Temptation is the pull of man's own evil thoughts and wishes. These evil thoughts lead to evil actions...."[3]

Sexually explicit thoughts are usually involuntary, at least initially. How a man handles these involuntary thoughts determines whether they become sin or not. If he welcomes such thoughts and embellishes them, they become sin. If he immediately repudiates them, they are nothing more than temptation. As someone has said, "A man can't keep the birds from flying over his head, but he can stop them from building a nest in his hair."

Principle #4: *Count the cost.* Do you think for a moment that King David would have committed adultery with Bathsheba if he had stopped to count the cost? Would he have considered the sexual pleasures of a stolen night worth the lifetime of sorrow he suffered? I think not.

God forgave David,[4] to be sure, and we remember him, not as an adulterer, but as a man after God's own heart. Unfortunately, life was not so merciful. David's sin set in motion a tragic series of events that nearly destroyed his family and his kingdom.

The child born from his illicit union with Bathsheba dies suddenly from a mysterious illness. Amnon, David's son, rapes his sister Tamar, creating a scandal in the palace. Two years later, Tamar's brother Absalom takes his revenge and murders Amnon. Finally, Absalom leads an armed rebellion against his father, David, driving him from Jerusalem and breaking his heart. And on the rooftop of the palace where David first lusted after Bathsheba, Absalom pitches a tent and "...[lies] with his father's concubines in the sight of all Israel."[5]

This tragic account is included in Scripture, not to satisfy some prurient curiosity we might have, but as a warning lest we make the same mistake.[6] Remember, no one lives in a vacuum. A man's sinful decisions will affect not only himself, but everyone he loves and cares about. Yes, God will forgive our sins, but how much better to allow Him to deliver us from temptation before we sin.

ACTION STEPS:

▼ THINK OF THE PEOPLE THAT YOU KNOW WHO HAVE COMMITTED SEXUAL SIN. NOW CONSIDER THE CONSEQUENCES THEY HAVE SUFFERED—THINGS LIKE GUILT, REGRET, SHAME, LOSS OF POSITION, DIVORCE, FINANCIAL SETBACK, AND SEXUALLY TRANSMITTED DISEASE.

▼ MEMORIZE PROVERBS 6:32: "BUT A MAN WHO COMMITS ADULTERY LACKS JUDGMENT; WHOEVER DOES SO DESTROYS HIMSELF."

THOUGHT FOR THE DAY:

"A chain of seemingly innocent choices became destructive, and it was my fault. Choice by choice by choice, each easier to make, each becoming gradually darker. And then my world broke—in the very area I had predicted I was safe...."[7]

Gordon MacDonald

SCRIPTURE FOR THE DAY:

"My son, keep my words and store up my commands within you. Keep my commands and you will live; guard my teachings as the apple of your eye. Bind them on your fingers; write them on the tablet of your heart...they will keep you from the adulteress, from the wayward wife with her seductive words."

PROVERBS 7:1-3,5

PRAYER:

LORD, DON'T LET ME GET AWAY WITH ANY SELF-DECEPTIVE RATIONALIZATION. CONFRONT ME, IN MY HEART OF HEARTS, WITH THE TRUTH ABOUT MY RELATIONSHIPS. CONVICT ME OF MY SINFUL DESIRES— UPROOT THEM. DELIVER ME FROM TEMPTATION, LEST IN MY SELFISHNESS I DESTROY MYSELF AND THOSE I LOVE. IN THE NAME OF JESUS I PRAY. AMEN.

[1]   Proverbs 7:1,5.
[2]   Job 31:1.
[3]   James 1:14-15 TLB.
[4]   2 Samuel 12:13.
[5]   2 Samuel 16:22.
[6]   1 Corinthians 10:4.
[7]   Gordon MacDonald, *Rebuilding Your Broken World* (Nashville: Oliver-Nelson Books, a division of Thomas Nelson, Inc., Publishers, 1988), p. 53.

CHAPTER 41

DEADLY SECRETS AND HEALING GRACE

In his book *Rebuilding Your Broken World*, Gordon MacDonald writes, "Studies suggest that more than half of American mid-life males live with at least one secret in the past of their personal lives, and these men believe its revelation would bring about catastrophic consequences for them and those close to them."[1]

If this is true, and my personal experience as a pastor and counselor seems to verify it, then there are a lot of hurting men out there.

Initially, a man's secret sin will be a source of deep distress. Hear King David as he describes the inner turmoil he experienced the year he tried to cover up his adulterous affair with Bathsheba. "When I kept silent," he says, "my bones wasted away through my groaning all day long. For day and night your [God's] hand was heavy upon me; my strength was sapped as in the heat of summer."[2]

And again he confesses, "My guilt has overwhelmed me like a burden too heavy to bear...I am bowed down and brought very low; all day long I go about mourning. My back is filled with searing pain; there is no health in my body. I am feeble and utterly crushed; I groan in anguish of heart."[3]

If you are living in secret sin, you know what David is talking about. Your heart hurts. You despise yourself. Shame has made you sick, and you have little or no energy. Weariness weighs you down, but sleep won't come. Fear eats at your belly. Depression dogs your days. You feel trapped and you are tempted to run away, but where can you go to escape yourself? Thoughts of suicide tempt you with promises of sweet oblivion, but fear of the eternal consequences stay your hand.

There is only one way to put an end to your torment, only one way to escape your prison of pain. Confess your sins and renounce them, come clean with God.

Although only God can forgive sin, I am convinced that secret sin can only be overcome by confessing it to another person as well as to God. Sin flourishes in the dark, it thrives in secret; but expose it to the light through honest confession to a fellow believer, and it withers and dies.

Let me offer a word of advice here. Choose your confessor carefully. He should be a mature believer, a man of integrity, trustworthy, compassionate, and nonjudgmental.

Not infrequently, I am asked by husbands guilty of sexual sin if they should tell their wives. While each situation must be considered on its own merits, as a general rule I think not. If a man's wife has absolutely no idea of his philandering, then he should think long and hard before he tells her. Why make her suffer for his sins? On the other hand, if she questions him, he must tell her the absolute truth. He must not lie to her.

God is long-suffering and merciful. More than anything, He wants to deliver you from your sinful trap. If you will voluntarily confess your sins and renounce them, God has no desire to make them public. However, if you persist in your clandestine ways, He has no choice but to expose your sins. Even then His intent is mercy rather than judgment. Above all, He wants to forgive your sins and deliver you from your self-made hell!

When Nathan the prophet finally confronted King David about his sinful affair with Bathsheba, it was both painfully humiliating and wonderfully liberating. It was humiliating in the sense that David's sin was now public knowledge. He could no longer pretend to be something he was not. It was liberating because he could stop pretending and throw himself on the mercies of God.

Hear David as he worships the Lord and celebrates his deliverance: "Then I acknowledged my sin to you and did not cover up my iniquity. I said, 'I will confess my transgressions to the LORD'—and you forgave the guilt of my sin."[4]

His sorrow has now been turned into joy, and he shouts aloud the praises of God his Savior. "Blessed is he whose transgressions are forgiven, whose sins are covered. Blessed is the man whose sin the LORD does not count against him and in whose spirit is no deceit."[5]

Be assured that your sins will find you out.[6] The only choice you have is in regard to how. You can confess your sin in a confidential setting or you can repeatedly cover it until God's only hope of redeeming you is to allow your sin to be revealed. How much better to voluntarily confess your sin in private rather than having it exposed in public?

To my knowledge there is no scriptural reason why your transgression need be made public if you have forsaken your sin, voluntarily confessed it, and made yourself accountable to a mature brother. On the other hand, if you persist in continuing your double life, then God has no choice but to allow your sin to become common knowledge in hopes of bringing you to repentance.

Remember, "He who conceals his sins does not prosper, but whoever confesses and renounces them finds mercy."[7]

ACTION STEPS:

▼ IF THERE IS SECRET SIN IN YOUR LIFE, CONFESS IT TO GOD RIGHT NOW AND RECEIVE HIS FORGIVENESS.

▼ MAKE YOURSELF ACCOUNTABLE TO YOUR PASTOR OR A TRUSTED CHRISTIAN BROTHER. CONFESS YOUR SECRET SIN TO THEM.

▼ MAKE WHATEVER CHANGES ARE NECESSARY TO CUT OFF ALL CONTACT WITH THE PERSONS AND PLACES WHERE YOUR SECRET SIN FLOURISHED.

THOUGHT FOR THE DAY:

"I thought of what might be called the underside of the church: those numberless people who walk into sanctuaries all over the world carrying their secrets behind bright clothing and forced smiles. They sing the songs, pray the prayers, listen to the sermons. And all the while the secrets fester within the private world causing either a constantly broken heart or a hardened heart. They come in fear of their secrets being exposed, and they quite likely go in fear that they will have to live this way for the rest of their lives. Believe me, the underside of the church is there, listening and watching to find out whether there is anyone with whom their secret might be safe if revealed."[8]

Gordon MacDonald

SCRIPTURE FOR THE DAY:

"Therefore confess your sins to each other and pray for each other so that you may be healed. The prayer of a righteous man is powerful and effective."

JAMES 5:16

PRAYER:

LORD, I CONFESS MY SECRET SIN. I NAME IT. I HAVE NO EXCUSES, NO SELF-JUSTIFYING RATIONALIZATIONS. IT WAS MY FAULT. I AM TO BLAME. FORGIVE ME, I PRAY, AND CHANGE ME. MAKE ME TRULY YOUR PERSON IN BOTH THOUGHT AND DEED. IN THE NAME OF JESUS I PRAY. AMEN.

1 Gordon MacDonald, *Rebuilding Your Broken World* (Nashville: Oliver-Nelson Books, a division of Thomas Nelson, Inc., Publishers, 1988), p. 72.
2 Psalm 32:3-4.
3 Psalm 38:4,6-8.
4 Psalm 32:5.
5 Psalm 32:1-2.
6 Numbers 32:23.
7 Proverbs 28:13.
8 Gordon MacDonald, *Rebuilding Your Broken World* (Nashville: Thomas Nelson Publishers, 1988), p. 67.

THE SIXTH CHARACTERISTIC OF A MAN OF VALOR IS

WISDOM

"Knowing that wisdom waits to be gathered, I will actively search her out. My past can never be changed, but I can change the future by changing my actions today. I will change my actions today! I will train my eyes and ears to read and listen to books and recordings that bring about positive changes in my personal relationships and a greater understanding of my fellowman. No longer will I bombard my mind with materials that feed my doubts and fears. I will read and listen only to what increases my belief in myself and my future."[1]

CHAPTER 42

A PRAYER FOR WISDOM

As the King of Israel, Solomon was the most powerful ruler in the world. His wealth and wisdom were legendary, inspiring visits from all manner of foreign dignitaries,[2] including the queen of Sheba.[3] Young men who aspired to royal service looked up to him as their model. Scholars suggest that his Proverbs were created as curriculum for their training. That being the case, the most important thing he could impart to them was the secret of his success.

As he pondered that responsibility, perhaps his thoughts returned to his own beginnings, to the time God appeared to him in a dream. "...God said, 'Ask for whatever you want me to give you.'"[4]

With insight beyond his years, Solomon asked, not for riches or power, but for wisdom. This pleased the Lord and He said, "'...I will give you a wise and discerning heart, so that there will never have been anyone like you, nor will there ever be. Moreover, I will give you what you have not asked for—both riches and honor—so that in your lifetime you will have no equal among kings.'"[5]

The wisdom Solomon received was a composite—"'...a discerning heart to govern...and to distinguish between right and wrong....'"[6] It was not long before his wisdom was put to the test. Two prostitutes came before him in a dispute about a baby. The facts were plain enough—each of them was the mother of a newborn infant. During the night one of the babies had died. Now each woman was claiming the living child as her own. There were no witnesses. It was one mother's word against the other's.

Then the king said,... "Cut the living child in two and give half to one and half to the other."

The woman whose son was alive was filled with compassion for her son and said to the king, "Please, my lord, give her the living baby! Don't kill him!"...

Then the king gave his ruling: "Give the living baby to the first woman. Do not kill him; she is his mother.'"

When all Israel heard the verdict the king had given, they held the king in awe, because they saw that he had wisdom from God to administer justice.[7]

Inspired, perhaps by such memories, Solomon counsels the young men of his day, "'Choose my instruction instead of silver, knowledge rather than choice gold, for wisdom is more precious than rubies, and nothing you desire can compare with her...For whoever finds [wisdom] finds life and receives favor from the LORD'"[8] As men charged with the responsibility to lead our families, our churches, and our communities, we too are in need of wisdom from above. Thankfully, God has promised it to every man who asks. "If any of you lacks wisdom, he should ask God, who gives generously to all...and it will be given to him."[9]

ACTION STEPS:

▼ IDENTIFY SOMEONE IN YOUR CIRCLE OF FRIENDS OR ASSOCIATES WHO DEMONSTRATES GODLY WISDOM. WHY DID YOU CHOOSE THIS PARTIC-ULAR PERSON? WHAT CHARACTER TRAITS OR ACTIONS CAUSED YOU TO CONCLUDE THAT HE WAS A WISE MAN? BE SPECIFIC.

▼ IF POSSIBLE, ARRANGE TO HAVE LUNCH OR TO GO FOR COFFEE WITH THIS MAN. SHARE THIS CHAPTER WITH HIM AND ASK HIM HOW HE MAKES WISE DECISIONS. ASK HIM WHO WAS HIS MENTOR OR MODEL.

▼ FOLLOWING YOUR MEETING, MAKE A LIST OF THE THINGS YOU LEARNED AND PLAN SPECIFIC WAYS TO INTEGRATE THOSE PRINCIPLES INTO YOUR OWN LIFE.

THOUGHT FOR THE DAY:

"Wisdom is your perspective on life, your sense of balance, your understanding of how the various parts and principles apply and relate to each other. It embraces judgment, discernment, comprehension. It is a gestalt or oneness, an integrated wholeness."[10]

Stephen R. Covey

SCRIPTURE FOR THE DAY:

*"To you, O men, I call out; I raise my voice to all mankind.
You who are simple, gain prudence; you who are foolish, gain understanding...
Choose my instruction instead of silver, knowledge rather than choice gold,
for wisdom is more precious than rubies, and nothing you desire can compare
with her...For whoever finds me finds life and receives favor from the LORD."*

PROVERBS 8:4-5,10-11,35

PRAYER:

LORD, GIVE ME THE DESIRE TO SEEK YOUR WISDOM AND THE

DISCIPLINE TO DO THOSE THINGS WHICH WILL PREPARE ME

TO RECEIVE IT. IN THE NAME OF JESUS I PRAY. AMEN.

1   Andy Andrews, *The Traveler's Gift* (Nashville: Thomas Nelson Publishers, 2002), pp. 48, 49.
2   1 Kings 4:34.
3   1 Kings 10:1-13.
4   1 Kings 3:5.
5   1 Kings 3:12-13.
6   1 Kings 3:9.
7   1 Kings 3:24-28.
8   Proverbs 8:10-11,35.
9   James 1:5.
10 Stephen R. Covey, *The Seven Habits of Highly Effective People* (New York: A Fireside Book published by Simon & Schuster, 1989), p. 109.

CHAPTER 43

THREE WAYS GOD IMPARTS WISDOM

The question before us is not, will the Lord give us wisdom? That's a given: "If any of you lacks wisdom, he should ask God, who gives generously to all...."[1] For us the question is, how does God impart His wisdom?

First, God reveals His wisdom through the Scriptures. They are filled with practical truths warning us against co-signing a note, idleness , reckless words, selfishness, dishonesty in business, and foolish companions, to name just a few. They also provide great principles, eternal truths, which become the core values that govern our lives. Principles like: "... 'seek first his [God's] kingdom and his righteousness, and all these things will be given to you as well.'"[2] Or, "Whoever finds his life will lose it, and whoever loses his life for my [Jesus'] sake will find it."[3]

A second way that God imparts His wisdom is through others. Proverbs 13:20 declares, "He who walks with the wise grows wise, but a companion of fools suffers harm."

Some years ago a dear friend of mine went through an extremely difficult time. The congregation where he served as senior pastor was unusually critical and finally forced him to resign. Although this situation was extremely painful for him and his family, not to mention the financial adversity it created, he never uttered an unkind word.

One day, while we were having coffee, I asked him how he managed to maintain such a positive attitude and such a pure spirit. Without a moment's hesitation he replied, "I've never been a bitter or vindictive person, and I'm not going to allow anyone to make me into something I'm not!"

In that instant I recognized that God was giving me special wisdom through the words and experience of my friend. Since that day I have had more than one occasion to act on the truth he imparted, and it has served me well, protecting me from the snare of the enemy.

A third way God imparts His wisdom is through the inner prompting of His Spirit. Throughout my years of ministry, I have faced a number of situations that were beyond my expertise. On such occasions I go to God in prayer. Like Solomon of old I pray, "'Give me wisdom and knowledge, that I may lead this people....'"[4]

Without fail, God answers my desperate prayer. Sometimes He speaks to me from the Scriptures, or through the counsel of a trusted friend, but more often than not His wisdom comes as a thought, a solution, a course of action. And once conceived it often seems so simple, so obvious, that I am tempted to discount His role in it. Yet a more spiritually sensitive part of me recognizes it as the wisdom of God.

Usually God does not answer my prayer while I am praying. I mean, I often leave the place of prayer without a clue as to what to do. Most often the answer comes when I least expect it, when I am not even thinking about the problem. Sometimes it comes as my first thought upon awaking in the morning, full blown and complete. At others times it comes to me while I am showering or when I am driving. I can only conclude that my mind needs to be at rest before God can impart His wisdom to me.

ACTION STEPS:

▼ REMEMBER A TIME WHEN GOD IMPARTED WISDOM TO YOU. HOW DID HE COMMUNICATE IT TO YOU? WAS IT IN ONE OF THE THREE WAYS I MENTIONED OR IN SOME OTHER WAY?

▼ IF YOU ARE FACING A CHALLENGING SITUATION OR AN IMPORTANT DECISION, SURRENDER IT TO GOD IN PRAYER RIGHT NOW. ASK HIM TO GIVE YOU THE WISDOM TO MAKE A WISE DECISION.

▼ OVER THE NEXT SEVERAL DAYS BE AWARE OF THE WAYS YOU RECEIVE INPUT TO RESOLVE THIS SITUATION. BE ESPECIALLY SENSITIVE TO THE PRESENCE OF GOD AT WORK IN YOUR LIFE AND MAKE NOTE OF IT.

THOUGHT FOR THE DAY:

"When a pond is greatly agitated by the breezes and the wind, one can throw in a pebble or even many pebbles and there is no noticeable effect. When a pond is perfectly at peace and one casts a pebble into it, the gentle waves spread in every direction till they reach even the farthest shore. When we are in the midst of a busy everyday life, so many thoughts go in and out of our minds and our hearts, we don't perceive the effect they are having upon us. But when we come to achieve a deeper inner quiet, then we are much more discerning. The way is open to follow even the most gentle leadings of the Spirit and to avoid even the most subtle deviations that are suggested either by the self or by the evil one."[5]

M. Basil Pennington

SCRIPTURE FOR THE DAY:

"For the LORD gives wisdom, and from his mouth come knowledge and understanding."

PROVERBS 2:6

PRAYER:

LORD, STILL MY OVERACTIVE MIND AND QUIET MY RAMBUNCTIOUS SPIRIT. MAKE ME SENSITIVE TO THE GENTLE PROMPTING OF YOUR SPIRIT THAT I MAY KNOW AND DO YOUR WILL. IN THE NAME OF JESUS I PRAY. AMEN.

---

[1] James 1:5.
[2] Matthew 6:33.
[3] Matthew 10:39.
[4] 2 Chronicles 1:10.
[5] M. Basil Pennington, *Centering Prayer,* quoted in *Disciplines for the Inner Life* by Bob Benson and Michael W. Benson (Waco: Word Books Publisher, 1985), p.164.

CHAPTER 44

A WORD TO THE WISE ABOUT FRIENDS

Every man needs a friend, someone in whom he can confide. There is simply no way to overstate the tremendous need he has to be really listened to, to be taken seriously, to be understood. Without that kind of relationship, he will never experience his full potential as a human being and a man of God.

According to Dr. Paul Tournier, the eminent Swiss psychiatrist and Christian thinker, "No one can develop freely in this world and find a full life without feeling understood by at least one person. Misunderstood, he loses his self-confidence, he loses his faith in life or even in God."[1]

Yet, few men have the kind of friendships where they can let their guard down and truly be themselves. The reasons are both cultural and experiential.

"According to Elliot Engel of North Carolina State, the male twosome is designed more for combat than comfort. Men are expected to compete, whether the setting is the tennis court or the law court."[2] Joel Block, a Long Island psychologist, concurs. He says the growing-up message programmed into men is "Show any weakness, and we'll clobber you with it."[3]

Those who manage to overcome these cultural hang-ups and build a friendship based on mutual trust, transparency, and vulnerability experience personal wholeness and a depth of self-knowledge uncommon among men. Yet, such a relationship is not without its risks. Not infrequently the man who enters into such a friendship finds his trust betrayed. He tells his friend of the difficulties he is experiencing with his supervisor, only to discover that his friend uses that information for his own advancement. Or he confides that he is having trouble with sex in his marriage and his friend "jokingly" replies, "Well, perhaps I ought to come over and help you out."

Such betrayal only reinforces his cultural training, and after one or two such experiences most men learn to keep their own counsel. Well it has been said that women start out as strangers and end up as sisters, while men start as strangers and end up as swordsmen.

Is there a solution, an answer, a way for us men to build deep and meaningful friendships without risking it all? Yes, but only if we will accept the counsel of Scripture. The wise man instructs us to choose our friends carefully. He writes, "A gossip betrays a confidence; so avoid a man who talks too much."[4]

Never trust a man who tells you another man's secret. If he betrays that man's confidence, he is likely to betray yours as well. Such a man reveals the things told to him in confidence as a way of proving his importance. The deepest issues of another man's life become the currency he uses to advance himself. Beware of such a friend.

The Bible says, "The purposes of a man's heart are deep waters, but a man of understanding draws them out."[5] In other words, a man's motives are not always as pure as they first appear. A wise man withholds judgment until he has had opportunity to make sure that his potential friend's actions match his words.

The real key to building a true friendship is caution—not suspicion, but caution. Give your new friend a small piece of your heart. If he treats it with respect and understanding, or better yet, reciprocates, then share a little more of yourself. In this way, you can build a genuine friendship without risking your whole heart at once. As Solomon observed, "A righteous man is cautious in friendship...."[6]

ACTION STEPS:

▼ CONSIDER THIS: IF YOU WERE TO DISCOVER THAT YOUR WIFE WAS HAVING AN AFFAIR OR YOUR TEENAGE SON IS DOING DRUGS, WHO COULD YOU TALK TO? WHO COULD YOU TELEPHONE IN THAT TERRIBLE MOMENT AND SHARE YOUR DEEPEST HURT?

▼ IF YOU CANNOT THINK OF ANYONE OTHER THAN YOUR PASTOR AND/OR SOME OTHER PROFESSIONAL, THEN YOU PROBABLY DO NOT HAVE THE KIND OF FRIENDSHIPS YOU NEED IN ORDER TO BECOME ALL THAT GOD

HAS CALLED YOU TO BE. EXAMINE YOUR LIFE TO SEE IF YOU CAN DETER-
MINE WHY YOU LACK THAT KIND OF IN-DEPTH RELATIONSHIP. BE SPECIFIC.

▼ MAKE A LIST OF THE CHANGES YOU ARE WILLING TO MAKE TO DEVELOP
THE KIND OF FRIENDSHIPS WE'VE BEEN TALKING ABOUT. BE SPECIFIC.

THOUGHT FOR THE DAY:

"I've heard these real friends called five-finger friends—those you can
count on the fingers of one hand. They are the kind of friends who are
there for you no matter what happens. And it goes without saying that
you are there for them as well. Many a person has been sustained in the
hour of personal tragedy by such a friend and across the course of a lifetime they will prove absolutely priceless."

Richard Exley

SCRIPTURES FOR THE DAY:

A friend loves at all times, and a brother is born for adversity.
PROVERBS 17:17

A man that hath friends must shew himself friendly:
and there is a friend that sticketh closer than a brother.
PROVERBS 18:24 KJV

A gossip betrays a confidence; so avoid a man who talks too much.
PROVERBS 20:19

PRAYER:

LORD, I AM A BLESSED MAN. YOU HAVE GIVEN ME SOME VERY SPECIAL
FRIENDS. IN MY DARKEST HOUR, THEY HAVE BEEN MY STRENGTH AND MY
SUPPORT. THEY HAVE STOOD WITH ME, BELIEVED IN ME WHEN I COULD NO
LONGER BELIEVE IN MYSELF. WITHOUT THEM I DON'T THINK I COULD
HAVE MADE IT. NOW I ASK YOU TO MAKE ME A FRIEND LIKE THAT TO
SOMEONE WHO NEEDS THE STRENGTH OF FRIENDSHIP IN THE
MIDNIGHT HOUR OF HIS LIFE. IN JESUS' NAME I PRAY. AMEN.

[1] Paul Tournier, *To Understand Each Other*, translated by John S. Gilmour (Richmond: John Knox Press, 1962), p. 29.
[2] Paul D. Robbins, "Must Men Be Friendless?" *Leadership* (Fall 1984, Volume V Number 4), p. 25.
[3] Ibid.
[4] Proverbs 20:19.
[5] Proverbs 20:5.
[6] Proverbs 12:26.

CHAPTER 45

RULES FOR HIRING

As I look back over nearly three decades of ministry, I realize that some of the best decisions I ever made were hiring decisions. By the same token, some of the worst mistakes I ever made were also hiring decisions. The only comfort I can find is in the knowledge that I am not alone. When comparing notes with my ministerial colleagues, they readily acknowledge similar experiences. For the most part, our mistakes are painfully clear in retrospect, but at the time we were convinced that our decisions were good ones. Since the success of almost any endeavor depends upon the people we work with, let me share some of things I've learned through the years.

Rule #1: *Don't hire a friend.* Although some people can manage the difficult task of being both friend and boss, most of us can't. One of the first persons I called to serve on my staff was a close friend, and although he was enormously talented, it was an impossible situation. When I needed to give managerial direction, I ended up making friendly suggestions. When he should have deferred to my decisions as his senior pastor, he appealed to our friendship. Finally, I was forced to ask for his resignation, and in the process, I lost a dear friend.

Rule #2: *Don't hire a primary leader to fill a supporting role.* By temperament and talent some of us are primary leaders, and some of us are support personnel. When you try to squeeze a primary leader into a supporting role, you limit his effectiveness and increase his level of frustration. The narrow confines of his supporting role are like a cage, and he will constantly beat his wings against the bars. If you are not careful, he will challenge your role as primary leader, and even if you successfully withstand his challenge, the resulting fallout will have long-term consequences.

Rule #3: *Don't plan on changing anyone after you hire them.* After several frustrating experiences, I have come to the conclusion that what you hire is what you get. You can train a person, but you cannot change them. I know because I've tried it more times than I would like to remember.

One pastor tells of hiring a brilliant man. "His resume was impressive. Both his educational achievements and his work experience were exceptional. He was articulate, creative, and possessed outstanding social skills."

Sounds great so far doesn't it? Who among us wouldn't want a person like that on our staff? But wait, there's more.

"Too late," this pastor continues, "I discovered that he was also lazy. If I gave him an assignment, he did it in record time, but that's as far as it went. He had little or no vision, no ideas of his own, and seemed intent on doing as little as possible."

I feel for that pastor because he's between a rock and a hard place. In a situation like that, he has only two choices—fire the man and deal with the consequences or live with him. Trying to change him is an absolute waste of time!

Rule #4: *Check his references.* Many hiring mistakes are made right here. If a man's resume looks good and he has an impressive interview, it's tempting to bypass the tedious task of checking his references. Even if you know the applicant personally, you cannot afford to ignore this time-consuming task. What he is socially and what he is as an employee may not be anything alike. Only someone who has worked with him can give you the scoop on his work habits.

One final word of caution. Don't accept his references at face value. Consider their relationship to him and what they may stand to gain by giving him a positive recommendation. Carefully weigh their comments against your own "gut" feeling.

Rule #5: *Attitude is more important than either talent or experience.* Most pastors I've talked with agree that nothing poisons staff relationships faster than a bad attitude. One smarting pastor referred to it as "staff infection," and he was only half kidding. Executives face the same thing with their management teams and readily admit that it is the bane of their jobs. Ask any man and they will tell you that there is not enough talent or experience to make up for a bad attitude. Nor is there any lack of experience or inaptitude that a great attitude cannot overcome.

A Princeton Seminary professor made a study of great preachers in an attempt to discover the secret of their effectiveness. "He noted their tremendous varieties of personalities and gifts. Then he asked the question, 'What do these outstanding pulpiteers all have in common besides their faith?' After several years of searching he found the answer. It was their cheerfulness."[1] They had a positive attitude.

The same thing is true in the workplace. A recent study by Telemetrics International determined that high achievers generally have a positive attitude, while low achievers usually have a poor attitude. As John Maxwell points out, "Usually the person who rises within an organization has a good attitude. The promotions did not give that individual an outstanding attitude, but an outstanding attitude resulted in promotions."[2]

ACTION STEPS:

▼ ALTHOUGH YOU MAY NOT BE IN A POSITION WHERE YOU ARE RESPONSIBLE FOR HIRING PEOPLE, THE PRINCIPLES CONTAINED IN THIS DEVOTIONAL MAY STILL SPEAK TO YOU. ASK YOURSELF, "WHAT IS GOD SAYING TO ME THROUGH THIS MATERIAL?"

▼ ARE YOU NOW, OR HAVE YOU EVER BEEN, RESPONSIBLE FOR HIRING PEOPLE? IF SO, MAKE A LIST OF YOUR HIRING GUIDELINES. HOW DO THEY COMPARE WITH THE GUIDELINES LISTED HERE?

▼ IF YOU HAD ONE PIECE OF ADVICE TO GIVE ON THIS MATTER, WHAT WOULD IT BE?

THOUGHT FOR THE DAY:

"A true and safe leader is likely to be one who has no desire to lead, but is forced into a position of leadership by the inward pressure of the Holy Spirit and the press of the external situation.... I believe it might be accepted as a fairly reliable rule of thumb that the man who is ambitious to lead is disqualified as a leader."[3]

A. W. Tozer

SCRIPTURE FOR THE DAY:

Like an archer who wounds at random is he who hires a fool or any passer-by.

PROVERBS 26:10

✠

PRAYER:

LORD, WHEN I THINK OF SOME OF THE CONSEQUENCES OF MY HIRING MISTAKES, I CRINGE. IT WASN'T JUST THE PRINCIPALS INVOLVED WHO GOT HURT, BUT INNOCENT BYSTANDERS AS WELL. HEAL THE WOUNDS MY MISTAKES HAVE CAUSED AND RESTORE THOSE WHO HAVE FALLEN. IN THE FUTURE MAKE ME MORE SENSITIVE TO YOUR DIRECTION AND LESS INTENT ON HAVING MY OWN WAY. IN THE NAME OF JESUS I PRAY. AMEN.

---

[1]   John C. Maxwell, *The Winning Attitude* (Nashville: Thomas Nelson Publishers, 1993), p. 35.
[2]   Ibid., p. 32.
[3]   Charles R. Swindoll, *Growing Strong in the Seasons of Life* (Portland: Multnomah Press, 1983), p. 359.

CHAPTER 46

WISDOM FOR LEADERS

According to Pastor Gordon MacDonald,[1] a leader has to deal with four basic types of people. First, there are the VIPs—the very important people. They are today's leaders and they help the primary leader accomplish his goals. By and large, they are self-sufficient men who require little of the leader other than direction, plus his respect and trust. From them he often receives strength and encouragement, for as the wise man writes, "As iron sharpens iron, so one man sharpens another."[2]

The second group is the VTPs—very trainable people. These are tomorrow's leaders. They are like the VIPs in talent and temperament, but they lack their experience and maturity. In order to achieve their full potential as men of God, they must be trained and discipled. Although their training requires a considerable amount of the leader's time and energy, it is time well spent. By investing himself in them, he multiplies his effectiveness.

The third group is the VNPs—very nice people. They like to be seen with the leader and count him as their friend. Being generous by nature, they make things like their lake house or condo in the mountains available for the leader's personal use. Their kindness is both a blessing and a burden. Even as it refreshes him, it also tempts him. The VNPs are fun to be with and make few demands, but, by the same token, they seldom make a significant contribution to the accomplishment of the leader's vision.

The fourth group is the VDPs—very draining people. They tend to be insecure persons with a long history of rejection. Because the leader is a compassionate man, they are drawn to him. Once he gives them his attention, they fasten themselves to him, demanding more and more of his life. While he must be available to them, lest he lose touch with the painful reality of human need, he must also guard himself; if he is not careful, their neediness will consume him.

In my work as a pastor, I found it not only helpful, but necessary to monitor my ministry in order to make sure I was investing myself where it would produce the greatest return for the Kingdom. For me, that meant investing in the lives of the VTPs—those men who will be tomorrow's leaders. Without a doubt, my greatest sense of fulfillment came in seeing them succeed. Through them my efforts are multiplied many times over.

In order to maintain my spiritual vitality, I had to balance my ministry relationships with nourishing friendships. These are reciprocal relationships in which each of us finds food for our soul. We exchange ideas, discuss the Scriptures, joke together, play together, and pray together—not as teacher and disciple, but as friend with friend. Spiritual ministry does take place, but it is a consequence of our friendship rather than a goal.

By monitoring both my ministry and my relationships, I am better able to fulfill my leadership responsibilities while maintaining a spiritually and emotionally healthy life. When I fall short of these high ideals, as I often do, God is faithful to both discipline and restore me.

ACTION STEPS:

▼ HOW DO YOU SEE YOURSELF? ARE YOU A PRIMARY LEADER, A VIP, A VTP, VNP, OR A VDP? EXPLAIN WHY YOU THINK OF YOURSELF IN THAT WAY. BE SPECIFIC.

▼ EXAMINE THE KEY RELATIONSHIPS IN YOUR LIFE TO SEE WHERE YOU ARE INVESTING YOURSELF. ARE YOUR PERSONAL INVESTMENTS IN THE LIVES OF OTHERS PRODUCING FRUIT, OR ARE YOU INVESTING INORDINATE AMOUNTS OF TIME FOR LITTLE OR NO RETURN?

▼ MAKE A LIST OF THE CHANGES YOU NEED TO MAKE IN ORDER FOR YOUR RELATIONSHIPS TO BECOME MORE SPIRITUALLY PRODUCTIVE? BE SPECIFIC.

THOUGHT FOR THE DAY:

"The trouble with a great many men is that they spread themselves out over too much ground. They fail in everything. If they would only put their life into one channel, and keep it, they would accomplish something. They make no impression, because they do a little work here and a little work there...lay yourselves on the altar of God, and then concentrate on some one work."[3]

D.L. Moody

SCRIPTURE FOR THE DAY:

"Instruct a wise man and he will be wiser still;
teach a righteous man and he will add to his learning."

PROVERBS 9:9

PRAYER:

LORD, FORGIVE ME FOR TRYING TO BE ALL THINGS TO ALL PEOPLE.
HELP ME TO LIVE A GOD-CENTERED LIFE RATHER THAN A NEED-
CENTERED ONE. FULFILL YOUR PURPOSES IN MY LIFE.
IN THE NAME OF JESUS I PRAY. AMEN.

[1]   "Anatomy of a Spiritual Leader" a conversation with Gordon MacDonald in *Leadership*, Fall 1984, Volume V Number 4, p. 111.
[2]   Proverbs 27:17.
[3]   Stanley and Patricia Gundry, eds., *The Wit and Wisdom of D.L. Moody* (Grand Rapids: Baker, 1982), pp. 63, 64.

CHAPTER 47

BEWARE OF
MISGUIDED ZEAL

Few things in life are more self-defeating than zeal without knowledge. It has claimed many a man, including presidents and kings, as well as military men of great renown. Numbered among its victims is Moses, the emancipator of Israel and few have fallen as far as he did.

Once a powerful prince in Pharaoh's palace, he was reduced to a fugitive tending sheep on the backside of the desert. Before his fall from grace he was a proud man, and why not? Among those who served in Pharaoh's courts none was as powerful as he, not in speech or in action.[1]

As you undoubtedly know, Moses was a Hebrew. Pharaoh's daughter adopted him and brought him to the palace after discovering him in a papyrus basket among some reeds along the bank of the Nile. His mother had hid him there rather than put him to death as Pharaoh's edict decreed.[2] For years it seemed he did everything he could to escape his Hebrew origins. He looked and dressed like an Egyptian prince, and he was educated in all the wisdom of the Egyptians. Everyone said he was destined for a distinguished political career. Then something happened. No one seems to know exactly what, but he changed. He became sullen, withdrawn.

When he was forty years old, he decided to visit his fellow Israelites.[3] While at the work site he saw one of them being mistreated by an Egyptian. In a fit of rage, he attacked the Egyptian and killed him.

The next day Moses returned only to discover two Hebrew slaves fighting. When he tried to intervene, the larger of the two men shoved him aside and said, "Who made you ruler and judge over us? Do you plan to kill me as you killed the Egyptian yesterday?"[4]

Moses tried to reason with him, tried to explain that God had placed him in a position of power so he could rescue them, but the man rejected the idea out of hand. By this time a crowd of slaves had gathered, so Moses appealed to them, but to no avail. They didn't trust him. As far as they were concerned he was a traitor to his own people.

Once Moses made his intentions known, his days were numbered. Pharaoh had ears everywhere and it was only a matter of time until he learned of Moses' clandestine meeting with the Hebrew slaves. As might be expected, he immediately issued orders to have Moses arrested and put to death. Fortunately, Moses learned of Pharaoh's intent and made his escape. He fled to Midian where he married the daughter of a priest and became a shepherd tending her father's sheep.

What sorely wounded Moses was not Pharaoh's reaction—that was to be expected—but the rejection he suffered at the hands of his own people. In retrospect, to have expected anything else was probably naive, but in his heart Moses was absolutely convinced that it was his destiny to free the Hebrew slaves. So sure was he that the God of his fathers, the God of Abraham, Isaac, and Jacob, had called him to set them free that he was willing to risk everything. When they refused to follow him, he lost his faith, not only in God, but in himself as well. From that moment forward he was a broken man.

What can we learn from all of this? First: *Planning must precede action.* Apparently Moses was so anxious to be about the Lord's business that he acted without a prepared plan. This is a common mistake among those who have zeal without knowledge. Having little patience for planning, and absolutely no time or interest in dealing with details, they rush ahead without considering the consequences. They are men of action, or perhaps I should say reaction, and they simply assume everyone else shares their vision and accepts their leadership—which is seldom the case. The resulting disaster often leaves them broken and embittered. As the wise man said, "A man's own folly ruins his life, yet his heart rages against the LORD."[5]

The second thing we learn is that *sincerity is not enough, nor is zeal or even good intentions.* Moses had all of these, and he still failed. Only God knows how much damage immature and overanxious believers have done, not only to the cause of Christ but to themselves as well. The secret of success in God's service is God's work in God's way in God's time!

And finally—the greatest lesson of all—*there is no failure God cannot redeem!* Moses got a second chance, and this time he succeeded. He challenged Egypt's military might and won; he confronted Pharaoh and negotiated the release of two million slaves, and then led them to freedom. Subsequently he gave them a system of government, a theocracy. He organized their religion, designed and built their place of worship, and defined God for them. For forty years, he was their spiritual father, their priest, their prophet, their general, and their prime minister. In addition, he penned the first five books of the Bible, including the Ten Commandments which, to this day, are the foundation for moral order in our society.

If you've failed, don't despair, not even if you've made a real mess of your life. "...God's gifts and his call are irrevocable."[6] That is to say, there is nothing you can do—no willful disobedience, no foolish mistake—which will cause God to revoke His call on your life. "For though a righteous man falls seven times, he rises again...."[7]

ACTION STEPS:

▼ EXAMINE THE WAY YOU MAKE DECISIONS. DO YOU THINK THINGS THROUGH OR DO YOU ALLOW YOUR UNBRIDLED ENTHUSIASM TO DISTORT YOUR JUDGMENT? DO YOU DISCUSS YOUR PLANS WITH YOUR WIFE OR ANYONE ELSE WHO MIGHT BE INVOLVED, OR DO YOU SIMPLY PRESENT THEM YOUR DECISION?

▼ IF YOU HAVE RECENTLY MADE A BAD DECISION, EXAMINE THE WHOLE PROCESS TO SEE WHAT YOU CAN LEARN FROM IT. WHERE DID YOU GO WRONG? WHAT WILL YOU DO DIFFERENT NEXT TIME?

▼ IF YOU HAVE RECENTLY MADE A WISE DECISION, EXAMINE THE WHOLE PROCESS TO SEE WHAT YOU CAN LEARN FROM IT. WHAT DID YOU DO RIGHT? WHAT PRINCIPLES WILL YOU USE THE NEXT TIME YOU HAVE AN IMPORTANT DECISION TO MAKE?

THOUGHT FOR THE DAY:

"Press on: Nothing in the world can take the place of persistence. Talent will not; nothing is more common than unsuccessful individuals with talent. Genius will not; unrewarded genius is almost a proverb. Education will not; the world is full of educated derelicts. Persistence and determination alone are omnipotent."[8]

Ray Kroc

SCRIPTURE FOR THE DAY:

"It is not good to have zeal without knowledge, nor to be hasty and miss the way."

PROVERBS 19:2

PRAYER:

LORD, I AM SO THANKFUL THAT YOU USED IMPERFECT MEN TO ACCOMPLISH YOUR PURPOSES. WITHOUT THEIR FAILURES, THEIR SUCCESSES WOULD INTIMIDATE ME. THEIR HUMANNESS, THEIR MISTAKES, GIVE ME HOPE. IF YOU COULD USE MEN LIKE THEM, THEN MAYBE YOU CAN USE A MAN LIKE ME TOO. USE ME FOR YOUR PURPOSES, O, LORD I PRAY. IN JESUS' NAME. AMEN.

---

[1] See Acts 7:22.
[2] See Exodus 2:2-6.
[3] See Acts 7:23-29.
[4] Acts 7:27,28.
[5] Proverb 19:3.
[6] Romans 11:29.
[7] Proverbs 24:16.
[8] Ray A. Kroc, *Grinding It Out* (New York: Berkley, 1978), p. 201.

CHAPTER 48

THE POWER OF AFFIRMATION

Few things in life are more powerful than the spoken word. It can heal or hurt, inspire or intimidate, comfort or crush. "The mouth of the righteous is a fountain of life," declares the wise man, "but violence overwhelms the mouth of the wicked."[1] Again he proclaims, "Reckless words pierce like a sword, but the tongue of the wise brings healing."[2]

As husbands and fathers, our words are especially powerful. This truth was driven home to me in a most painful way some years ago. Brenda and I were sharing on a deeper level than had heretofore been possible, when suddenly she began to sob. Through her tears she related an incident that took place nearly thirty years earlier. Although I had long since forgotten it, the mere memory of my words, three decades later, still had the power to make her cry.

Carelessly, I had said some hurtful, manipulative thing, as young men often do, and then had forgotten about it. For me it was a thing of the past, over and done. But Brenda hadn't forgotten; perhaps she couldn't forget. My reckless words had sorely wounded her. They had shaped the way she saw herself and our relationship, and now thirty years later, she still lived with the pain of their wounding.

Belatedly, I apologized and received her forgiveness, but nothing I did now could undo the wounds my reckless words had caused. Like water spilled on the ground which cannot be recovered, my words could not be taken back. With heartfelt sincerity I promised her that with God's help, I would carefully guard the things I said in the future.

Even as a reckless word wounds, so a well-spoken word gives life. It nourishes the soul, encourages the spirit, and affirms a person's worth.

The words of a parent are especially powerful, even prophetic. What a father believes about his children is important, but it is of limited benefit if he does not express it. When he speaks it, something almost magical happens. His words become a mirror, enabling his children to see themselves as he sees them. Not infrequently the things he sees—the character strengths he affirms, the gifts and talents he identifies, the future possibilities he envisions—give substance to his children's own secret dreams. His words become the first tangible evidence that their dreams are truly possible.

Some years ago, a group of undergraduates at the University of Wisconsin formed an all male literary club. There were some brilliant young men in the club with real literary talent, and they were determined to bring out the best in each other. At each meeting, one of them would read a story or essay he had written, and the others would critique it. They were merciless. Each manuscript was picked apart, no punches were pulled. To their way of thinking it was the only way to really develop their talent.

When the coeds heard about the club, they naturally formed one of their own. They too read their manuscripts aloud and offered constructive criticism, but it was criticism of a much gentler nature. Instead of focusing on the weaknesses of each manuscript, they looked for positive things to say. All efforts, however feeble, were encouraged.

The impact of each approach was not fully realized until several years later when an alumnus made an analysis of his classmates' careers. Not one of those bright young men had made a literary reputation of any kind. The coed club, on the other hand, had given rise to half a dozen successful writers, some of national prominence, including Marjorie Kinnan Rawlings, author of The Yearling.[3] Coincidence? I think not. The amount of raw talent was much the same in both groups. But while the coeds affirmed one another's talent, the men, with their penchant for merciless criticism, promoted self-doubt.

ACTION STEPS:

▼ EXAMINE YOUR SPEECH. WHAT KIND OF EMOTIONAL CLIMATE DO
YOU CREATE WITH YOUR WORDS? DO THE REMARKS YOU MAKE
ENCOURAGE OR INTIMIDATE YOUR CO-WORKERS, YOUR SPOUSE, AND
YOUR CHILDREN?

▼ ASK YOUR WIFE AND CHILDREN TO LIST FIVE ENCOURAGING THINGS
YOU HAVE SAID TO THEM IN THE LAST SEVEN DAYS. IF THEY CANNOT
REMEMBER THAT MANY, THEN MAKE A POINT OF BEING MORE AFFIRMING.

THOUGHT FOR THE DAY:

"Every man must be persuaded, even if he is in rags, that he is
immensely, immensely important. Everyone must respect him and
make him respect himself, too.... Give him great, great hopes. He
needs them, especially if he is young. Spoil him. Yes, make him
grow proud."[4]

Ugo Betti

SCRIPTURE FOR THE DAY:
The mouth of the righteous is a fountain of life,
but violence overwhelms the mouth of the wicked.

PROVERBS 10:11

PRAYER:

LORD, FORGIVE ME, FOR I HAVE SINNED WITH MY LIPS.

HOW I WISH I COULD TAKE BACK THE HURTFUL THINGS

I'VE SAID—CARELESS WORDS SPOKEN WITHOUT THINKING,

HARSH WORDS SPOKEN OUT OF HURT, SPITEFUL WORDS

SPOKEN IN ANGER. O LORD, DO WHAT I CANNOT DO.

HEAL THE WOUNDS I HAVE CAUSED AND RESTORE THAT WHICH

I HAVE DESTROYED. IN THE NAME OF JESUS I PRAY. AMEN.

[1] Proverbs 10:11.
[2] Proverbs 12:18.
[3] Arthur Gordon, *A Touch of Wonder* (Old Tappan: Fleming H. Revell, 1974), pp. 51, 52.
[4] Ugo Betti, "The Burnt Flower Bed" quoted in *No Longer Strangers* by Bruce Larson, (Waco: Word Company), p. 56.

CHAPTER 49

THE WISDOM OF PRAYER

"The 1992 report of the National Research Council says the United States is now the most violent of all industrialized nations.... For example the U.S. homicide rate for 15- to 24-year-old males is 7 times higher than Canada's and 40 times higher than Japan's. The U.S. has one of the highest teenage pregnancy rates, the highest teen abortion rate, and the highest level of drug use among young people in the developed world. Youth suicide has tripled in the past 25 years, and a survey of more than 2,000 Rhode Island students, grades six through nine, found that two out of three boys and one of two girls thought it 'acceptable for a man to force sex on a woman' if they had been dating for six months or more."[1]

Like many of us, criminologist James Q. Wilson wanted to know where America had gone wrong, so he set out to research the history of crime in America. In the process he stumbled on a historical fact he had not noticed before. The decrease in crime in the nineteenth century followed a widespread religious revival known as the Second Great Awakening. Repentance and renewal spread across the country, bringing moral reform. Once more American society came to respect the values of sobriety, hard work, self-restraint—what sociologists call the Protestant ethic.[2]

Then came the twentieth century, and by the 1920s and 1930s a host of new ideas were challenging the prevailing moral and religious values. Darwin's theory of evolution led people to see all things, including morality, as being in flux. The philosophy of logical positivism, asserted a radical distinction between facts (which could be scientifically proven) and values (which positivism held were mere expressions of feeling, not objective truth), causing many people to conclude that morality was relative and personal. As a result, by the 1960s, America was experiencing a crisis of moral authority, eroded belief in objective moral norms, the sexual revolution, and a spiraling crime rate.

As Chuck Colson so succinctly puts it, "The lesson of history is clear: When Christian belief is strong, the crime rate falls; when Christian belief weakens, the crime rate climbs. Widespread religious belief creates a shared social ethic that acts as a restraint on the dark side of human nature."[3]

This is not a new thought. The author of Proverbs first expressed it thousands of years ago: "Righteousness exalts a nation, but sin is a disgrace to any people."[4]

Two hundred years ago John Adams said, "Our constitution was made only for a moral and religious people. It is wholly inadequate for the government of any other."[5]

After studying two thousand years of Western civilization, historians Will and Ariel Durant concluded, "There is no significant example in history...of a society successfully maintaining moral life without the aid of religion."[6]

Congress can pass a massive anti-crime bill if it chooses. New tax dollars can put thousands more law enforcement officers on the streets. Judges can hand down harsh sentences for repeat offenders and hundreds of new prisons can be built to handle all the criminals, but if America does not return to her moral and spiritual roots, it will all be in vain.

The root cause of America's social dilemma is spiritual and the answer is prayer. Second Chronicles 7:14 declares, "If my people, who are called by my name, will humble themselves and pray and seek my face and turn from their wicked ways, then will I hear from heaven and will forgive their sin and will heal their land."

ACTION STEPS:

▼ FAMILIARIZE YOURSELF WITH ORGANIZATIONS LIKE FOCUS ON THE FAMILY'S CITIZENS' COUNCIL AND THE CHRISTIAN COALITION. PRAY ABOUT BECOMING ACTIVELY INVOLVED.

▼ FAMILIARIZE YOURSELF WITH THE SPIRITUAL TRUTHS OF AMERICAN HISTORY BY READING BOOKS LIKE *THE LIGHT AND THE GLORY* BY PETER MARSHALL AND DAVID MANUEL (FLEMING H. REVELL), AND *AMERICA'S GOD AND COUNTRY ENCYCLOPEDIA OF QUOTATIONS* COMPILED BY WILLIAM J. FEDERER (FAME). READ *A DANCE WITH DECEPTION* BY CHARLES COLSON (WORD) TO BECOME INFORMED ON CURRENT ISSUES.

▼ ORGANIZE A MEN'S PRAYER GROUP TO PRAY FOR OUR NATION.

THOUGHT FOR THE DAY:

"It was not until I went into the churches of America and heard her pulpits flame with righteousness that I understood her greatness.... Religion is indispensable to the maintenance of republican institutions...."

Alexis de Tocqueville

SCRIPTURES FOR THE DAY:

Righteousness exalts a nation, but sin is a disgrace to any people.

PROVERBS 14:34

"O Lord, the great and awesome God, who keeps his covenant of love with all who love him and obey his commands, we have sinned and done wrong. We have been wicked and have rebelled; we have turned away from your commands and laws...Now, our God, hear the prayers and petitions of your servant.... We do not make requests of you because we are righteous, but because of your great mercy. O Lord, listen! O Lord, forgive! O Lord, hear and act! For your sake, O my God, do not delay...."

DANIEL 9:4-5, 17-19

PRAYER:

LORD JESUS, FORGIVE US FOR WE HAVE SINNED. AS A NATION WE ARE GREEDY AND IMMORAL. WE ARE HEDONISTIC AND MATERIALISTIC, ARROGANT AND UNREPENTANT. HEAR THE CRY OF YOUR PEOPLE AND FORGIVE OUR SINS. HEAL OUR NATION AND RESTORE OUR NATIONAL CHARACTER. IN YOUR HOLY NAME I PRAY. AMEN.

1 Thomas Lickona, "The Return of Character Education," *Educational Leadership*, November 1993, pp. 6, 9.
2 Charles Colson with Nancy R. Pearcey, *A Dance with Deception* (Dallas: Word Publishing, 1993), p. 189.
3 Ibid., p. 190.
4 Proverbs 14:34.
5 William J. Federer, *America's God and Country Encyclopedia of Quotations* (Coppel, TX: Fame Publishing, Inc.), p. __.
6 Colson and Pearcey, pp. 195, 196.

CHAPTER 50

THE WISDOM OF
THE WORD

While kneeling in prayer, the Scripture reference Isaiah 41:9 sprang into my mind as clearly as any thought I have ever had. With an effort I dismissed it and returned to my prayers. Almost immediately it returned, and once more I thrust it from my mind. By concentrating I was able to focus on my prayers, but if I relaxed my stern self-control for even a moment, the thought returned, clearer and more insistent than ever.

Belatedly, I decided that God might be trying to tell me something so I opened my Bible to Isaiah 41. Beginning at verse 9 I read, "...'You are my servant; I have chosen you and have not rejected you. So do not fear, for I am with you; do not be dismayed, for I am your God. I will strengthen you and help you; I will uphold you with my righteous right hand. All who rage against you will surely be ashamed and disgraced; those who oppose you will be as nothing and perish. Though you search for your enemies, you will not find them. Those who wage war against you will be as nothing at all. For I am the LORD, your God, who takes hold of your right hand and says to you, Do not fear; I will help you.'"[1]

At the time I found the passage encouraging, but hardly earth-shattering. I promptly forgot it, never realizing that in a few weeks I would be clinging to it for dear life. In fact, in the dark days ahead it would become my hope, my source of strength.

Here's what happened. With absolutely no warning, I was publicly dismissed from my position as associate pastor. That was bad enough in and of itself, but it was just the latest in a continuing series of crises in our lives. Just weeks earlier we had cut our vacation short and rushed home to be with Brenda's mother as she underwent surgery to remove a grapefruit-sized tumor. Of course, we feared the worst, and although no one uttered the "C" word, it hung over us like a cloud. When the doctors informed us that the surgery was successful and the tumor was not malignant, we experienced euphoric relief. Imagine our dismay when two days later they told us her ovaries were cancerous.

With God's help we fought our way through the frightening possibilities that raised and tried to prepare ourselves for the trauma of radiation therapy. Now, on top of everything else, I was unemployed and without any immediate prospects of a new position. Still, as I told Brenda, we had nine years' experience in the ministry, and I figured it was just a matter of time before we were called to a new church.

While Brenda concentrated on homemaking and taking care of our daughter, Leah, I began sending out resumes. Before long I had more than thirty in the mail, and I was sure we would receive a call to a new congregation any day. Unfortunately, the weeks stretched into months without a single positive response, and my earlier optimism gave way to bouts of depression. I even had days when I seriously doubted that there was any place for me in the ministry.

Sometimes I would lay awake in the dead of night wondering what the future held. Brenda's mother was deathly ill from the radiation treatments, and I seriously doubted if she was going to make it. Statistically, she didn't seem to have much of a chance. Ovarian cancer is fatal 95 percent of the time. Brenda and I didn't discuss her mother's situation, but I could tell she was fighting fears of her own.

As our circumstances grew more desperate, my depression deepened. In anger I railed at God. Why had He abandoned us? Why didn't He answer our prayers? Why didn't He intervene in our behalf? Well do I remember telling Him that He wasn't much of a Father, that I was just a man, but I would never treat my daughter the way He was treating us.

Somewhere in the midst of that tirade the Holy Spirit reminded me of Isaiah 41. With trembling hands I opened my Bible and turned to the book of Isaiah. Finding the 41st chapter I begin to read. Through tear-blurred eyes I made out the words...God's word to me, to us! "...'do not fear, for I am with you; do not be dismayed, for I am your God...those who oppose you will be as nothing and perish. Though you search for your enemies, you will not find them....'"[2]

Then it hit me. Months ago, before I had any idea I would need a word from the Lord, God had given me this passage. Before I had even known enough to ask, God had already answered my prayer.[3] Armed with the promise of the Father, I now faced the future with renewed hope. I had nothing to fear, for God was my shield.

Our circumstances did not change immediately, but our attitude did. In time, we were invited to become pastors of the Church of the Comforter in Craig, Colorado, where we served for more than five years. From there, we went to Christian Chapel in Tulsa, Oklahoma, where we enjoyed more than twelve years of fruitful ministry. And best of all Brenda's mother beat the odds. It has now been nearly thirty years since she completed her radiation treatments, and the doctors have never been able to find another trace of cancer in her body.

Well did God say it: "Though you search for your enemies, you will not find them. Those who wage war against you will be as nothing at all. For I am the LORD, your God, who takes hold of your right hand and says to you, Do not fear; I will help you."[4]

ACTION STEPS:

▼ CAN YOU REMEMBER A TIME WHEN GOD MADE SOME PASSAGE OF SCRIPTURE ESPECIALLY ALIVE FOR YOU? GO BACK AND REREAD THAT PASSAGE AND SPEND A FEW MINUTES RELIVING THAT EXPERIENCE.

▼ MAKE A LIST OF SOME OF YOUR FAVORITE SCRIPTURES, THE ONES THAT HAVE BEEN PARTICULARLY HELPFUL TO YOU ACROSS THE YEARS.

▼ MAKE IT A POINT TO SHARE AT LEAST ONE OF YOUR SCRIPTURES WITH YOUR WIFE OR A BROTHER IN THE LORD. INVITE THEM TO SHARE ONE OF THEIR FAVORITE PASSAGES AS WELL.

THOUGHT FOR THE DAY:

"Do not let it be imagined that one must remain silent about one's feelings of rebellion in order to enter into dialogue with God. Quite the opposite is the truth: it is precisely when one expresses them that a dialogue of truth begins...By giving expression to his reproaches he becomes more sincere—and the dialogue can begin."[5]

Paul Tournier

SCRIPTURE FOR THE DAY:

"Every word of God is flawless; he is a shield to those who take refuge in him."

PROVERBS 30:5

✝

PRAYER:

LORD, YOU ARE MY REFUGE AND MY STRENGTH, A VERY PRESENT HELP IN THE TIME OF TROUBLE. I THANK YOU FOR YOUR WORD, WHICH HAS GUIDED AND SUSTAINED ME IN THE DARK HOURS WHEN IT SEEMED MY FAITH WOULD FAIL. MAY I CONTINUE TO HIDE IT IN MY HEART AGAINST THE DIFFICULT DAYS AHEAD. IN THE NAME OF JESUS I PRAY. AMEN.

---

[1]   Isaiah 41:9-13.
[2]   Isaiah 41:10-12.
[3]   See Isaiah 65:24.
[4]   Isaiah 41:12-13.
[5]   Paul Tournier, *The Meaning of Persons* quoted in "Reflections: On Life's Most Critical Questions" by Paul Tournier (New York: Harper & Row Publishers, 1976), pp. 113, 114.

CHAPTER 51

TO KNOW GOD IS
TO TRUST HIM

Nothing is more important than what a man believes about God. How he perceives Him will determine, to a significant degree, what he believes about himself and how he relates to others. It will also define his interpretation of life and the meaning of events. Never is his understanding of God more critical than in times of personal crisis. Consider, for example, the case of Judas Iscariot.

"When Judas, who had betrayed [Jesus], saw that Jesus was condemned, he was seized with remorse and returned the thirty silver coins to the chief priests and the elders. 'I have sinned,' he said, 'for I have betrayed innocent blood.'

'What is that to us?' they replied. 'That's your responsibility.'

"So Judas threw the money into the temple and left. Then he went away and hanged himself."[1]

Judas clearly understood the magnitude of his sin, but he severely underestimated the grace of God. He could not live with the evil thing he had done; worse yet, he could not believe that God would forgive him. To his way of thinking death was his only way out. It was both an escape and a desperate attempt to atone for his sin.

Judas's case is especially tragic because he had the benefit of spending three years with Jesus. He had heard His teachings, witnessed His miracles, and seen His redemptive love in action. How could he ever forget the woman caught in the very act of adultery or the words of Jesus when He said to her, "'...neither do I condemn you...Go now and leave your life of sin'"?[2]

I can only conclude that the magnitude of Judas's treachery was so great that his shameful guilt rendered these truths unreal. He remembered them no doubt, for who could ever forget, but to his way of thinking they had absolutely nothing to do with him. Tragically, he believed death at his own hand was somehow more merciful than the grace of God. What Judas believed about God determined his eternal fate in that critical hour.

David, on the other hand, never doubted the mercy of God, no matter how great his sin. Whatever his sin, whether it was adultery or murder or prideful disobedience in numbering Israel's fighting men, David threw himself upon the mercies of God. Hear him as he cries, "...'I have sinned greatly.... I am in deep distress. Let us fall into the hands of the LORD, for his mercy is great....'"[3]

To David's way of thinking, God's grace was always greater than his sin. As a result, we remember him not as an adulterer or a murderer, but as the sweet psalmist of Israel, a man after God's own heart and the earthly forefather of our Lord and Savior, Jesus Christ.

The defining difference between David and Judas was their image of God. To David's way of thinking, "The LORD is a refuge for the oppressed, a stronghold in times of trouble."[4] He declared, "Those who know your name will trust in you, for you, LORD, have never forsaken those who seek you."[5]

To know God's name is not merely to know His title or what to call Him. A person's name, in the biblical sense, is the expression of his character, his nature. What David was saying then is that those of us who know God's character will put our trust in Him. Or as Solomon says, "The name of the LORD is a strong tower; the righteous run to it and are safe."[6]

ACTION STEPS:

▼ COPY HEBREWS 11:11, PSALM 145:17, DEUTERONOMY 4:31, EXODUS 34:6, ROMANS 4:21, EPHESIANS 3:20, PSALM 23:4, AND EXODUS 3:7-8 ONTO 3 X 5 CARDS AND CARRY THEM WITH YOU IN YOUR POCKET OR IN YOUR BRIEFCASE.

▼ MAKE A POINT OF READING THROUGH THEM TWO OR THREE TIMES A DAY FOR SEVERAL DAYS. MEDITATE ON THEM UNTIL YOUR HEART AND MIND ARE SATURATED WITH THEIR TRUTH.

▼ IDENTIFY ANY SITUATIONS IN YOUR LIFE TO WHICH THOSE SCRIPTURES APPLY. WHAT IS GOD SAYING TO YOU ABOUT THESE SITUATIONS? BE SPECIFIC.

THOUGHT FOR THE DAY:

"I know God is faithful so I trust Him (Hebrews 11:11).

I know God is loving so I trust Him (Psalm 145:17).

I know God is merciful so I trust Him (Deuteronomy 4:31).

I know God is compassionate so I trust Him (Exodus 34:6).

I know God is able so I trust Him (Ephesians 3:20).

I know God is near so I trust Him (Psalm 23:4).

I know God is aware of my situation so I trust Him (Exodus 3:7).

I know God is involved in my situation so I trust Him (Exodus 3:8)."

A Private Journal

SCRIPTURE FOR THE DAY:

The LORD said, "I have indeed seen the misery of my people in Egypt. I have heard them crying out because of their slave drivers, and I am concerned about their suffering. So I have come down to rescue them from the hand of the Egyptians and to bring them up out of that land into a good and spacious land, a land flowing with milk and honey...."

EXODUS 3:7-8

PRAYER:

LORD, YOU ARE MY STRENGTH, MY HOPE, AND MY REFUGE, A VERY PRESENT HELP IN THE TIME OF TROUBLE. I COME BOLDLY INTO YOUR PRESENCE, NOT BECAUSE OF WHO I AM, BUT BECAUSE OF WHO YOU ARE. I TRUST YOU WITH MY LIFE, WITH ALL THAT I AM. IN THE NAME OF JESUS I PRAY. AMEN.

---

1   Matthew 27:3-5.
2   John 8:11.
3   2 Samuel 24:10,14.
4   Psalm 9:9.
5   Psalm 9:10.
6   Proverbs 18:10.

THE SEVENTH CHARACTERISTIC OF A MAN OF VALOR IS

GODLY COMPASSION

"What does love look like?
It has hands to help others.
It has feet to hasten to the poor and needy.
It has eyes to see misery and want.
It has ears to hear the sighs and sorrow of men.
That is what love looks like."[1]

ST. AUGUSTINE

CHAPTER 52

BLUE COLLAR CHRISTIANITY[2]

In our home, Christianity wasn't a moral code, church membership, or a way of behaving in public. It was a lifestyle—love with its sleeves rolled up! If there was a job to do, we did it. If there was a need, we did our best to meet it. Pleasing God and serving others was our life's goal.

Once when I was still in elementary school, we came out of church after prayer meeting, on a Wednesday night, and saw a transient family in a beat-up old car, parked in front of the church. They looked tired and a hungry baby whimpered from the broken-down backseat. Even as a child, I could see the hollow look in their eyes, the quiet desperation that had prematurely aged their faces, leaving them flat and empty. They were good people, just down on their luck and too proud to ask for help. Still, it was obvious that they were hoping some of the Lord's people would have compassion on them.

Dad did. He walked right over to the driver's side of the car, stuck out his hand, and introduced himself. Then he asked, "Have you had supper?"

Though he was obviously embarrassed, I will never forget what that desperate father said. Nodding toward the children in the backseat he muttered, "We ain't et since yesterday."

Without missing a beat, Dad said, "That's our car up ahead. If you will follow us home, Irene will make supper for you. And if you don't have a place to spend the night, you can stay with us."

We didn't have much, as I recall, but the folks were always more than willing to share what little we had. Mother put together a simple meal of homemade bread, fried potatoes, and ham. I followed Dad down into the half-finished basement where we collected two quarts of home canned peaches for desert. As we ascended the stairs, I distinctly remember the sound of ham sizzling in the skillet. Since that night it's always sounded like love to me—God's love.

Another time, Dad remodeled a small house for a young widow and her two children. Her husband, Merl, had died suddenly of a brain tumor, leaving her with almost nothing. Following the funeral, she was forced to move into more affordable housing. The only thing she could find was a small house that was in desperate need of repair.

When Dad learned of her situation, he offered to help. Night after night, for several weeks, we two boys and Mom accompanied him as he repaired the plumbing, put in new wiring, built cupboards for the kitchen and repainted inside and out. Finally, he was finished and that grieving family had a small but comfortable place to call home. More importantly, they knew they were not alone, God had not forgotten them! That too is love—the blue collar kind.

Thanks to the example set for me by my parents, I entered the ministry with a commitment to practical Christianity. It was a good thing, too, for my first church was a small congregation in the south-eastern Colorado town of Holly with a population of less than one thousand. It was my job to clean the church, take care of the yard, shovel the walks in winter and, in general, maintain the place. Oh yes, I was also expected to preach three times a week, teach a Sunday school class, lead the singing, visit the sick, and bury the dead.

For the most part, my congregation consisted of down-to-earth people—farmers and ranchers who had weathered drought and dust, tornadoes and hail, blizzards and tough times—and they weren't overly impressed with big words or theological concepts. Their Christianity was of a more practical kind. Almost immediately I realized that my effectiveness lay not so much in the sermons I preached, but in the way I lived and how I loved. If I hadn't been a "blue-collar Christian," they would not have listened to a thing I had to say.

Soon I found myself driving a grain truck at harvest time and helping round up the cattle in the fall. In between, I spent several afternoons with a wonderful old woman named Pearl who was dying of stomach cancer. I would sit with her at the kitchen table in the ranch house, drinking coffee while she told me how she and her husband had homesteaded the place. From her I learned the power of presence, the ministry of just being there, and the holy art of living until we die. It was the beginning of a special relationship with her family that continues to this day.

I remember another elderly lady, a long time member of the church, whose health no longer permitted her to attend services. Her name was Sister Patterson and she lived across the alley, just south of the church. Each week I would go to her home and share the midweek Bible study with her. It seemed the least I could do, but she made me feel as if I were doing her a special favor. Today I suppose we would send her a CD of the service, but somehow I don't think it would be the same. Not for me anyway, for without those weekly visits my theology of the Church would be incomplete. Church is far more than what happens on Sunday. It's a holy fellowship where people really care about each other. Sister Patterson taught me that.

At its heart Christianity is not merely sermon and song, but kindness—a cup of cold water in His name. Sometimes it means giving comfort in the moment of tragedy or encouragement to a family in crisis. At other times, we help celebrate a fortieth birthday or a twenty-fifth wedding anniversary. Just doing what we can to let our lights shine. Some places that's called church. I call it godly compassion or "blue collar Christianity."

ACTION STEPS:

▼ THINK OF SOMEONE YOU KNOW WHO EXHIBITS GODLY COMPASSION. MAKE A LIST OF SOME OF THE THINGS THEY DO.

▼ HOW COMPASSIONATE ARE YOU? RATE YOURSELF ON A SCALE OF ONE TO TEN, WITH TEN BEING THE HIGHEST.

▼ LIST SEVERAL STEPS YOU CAN TAKE TO BECOME MORE COMPASSIONATE. BE SPECIFIC.

THOUGHT FOR THE DAY:

"Somewhere in the world there should be a society consciously and deliberately devoted to the task of seeing how love can be made real, and demonstrating love in practice."[3]

Dr. Elton Trueblood

SCRIPTURE FOR THE DAY:

"Then the King will say to those on his right, 'Come, you who are blessed by my Father; take your inheritance, the kingdom prepared for you since the creation of the world. For I was hungry and you gave me something to eat, I was thirsty and you gave me something to drink, I was a stranger and you invited me in, I needed clothes and you clothed me, I was sick and you looked after me, I was in prison and you came to visit me.'
"Then the righteous will answer him, 'Lord, when did we see you hungry and feed you, or thirsty and give you something to drink? When did we see you a stranger and invite you in, or needing clothes and clothe you? When did we see you sick or in prison and go to visit you?'
"The King will reply, 'I tell you the truth, whatever you did for one of the least of these brothers of mine, you did for me.'"

MATTHEW 25:34-40

PRAYER:

LORD JESUS, YOU KNOW HOW I LOVE TO MINISTER FOR YOU WHEN I AM IN THE LIMELIGHT. HELP ME TO SERVE YOU WITH THE SAME PASSION WHEN IT COMES TO FEEDING THE HUNGRY, VISITING THE PRISONERS, OR ANY OTHER KIND OF UNGLAMOROUS, BEHIND-THE-SCENES MINISTRY. IN YOUR HOLY NAME I PRAY. AMEN.

[1] St. Augustine, quoted in *Dawnings, Finding God's Light in the Darkness,* edited by Phyllis Hobe (New York: Guideposts Associates, Inc., 1981), p. 96.

[2] Much of the material for this chapter was first published in *Blue Collar Christianity* by Richard Exley (Tulsa: Honor Books, 1989), pp. 13-18.

[3] Gordon C. Hunter, *When the Walls Come Tumblin' Down* (Waco: Word Books Publisher, 1970), p. 26.

CHAPTER 53

CARING ENOUGH TO LISTEN

By nature, men are problem solvers. It's not something we have to think about, it just comes with the territory. Show us something that is broken, and we will try to fix it. Share a problem with us, and immediately we will try to solve it. While that masculine attribute equips us to function in the workplace, it can be a painful liability in our marriage.

When a woman is hurting, when she's had a hard day or suffered an unsettling disappointment, the last thing she wants is advice or a quick fix. Not realizing this, a man can get in over his head before he even realizes what is happening.

Take Bill for example. When Joyce arrives home after an exhausting day at the office and begins sharing her frustrations, he listens just long enough to assess the situation before he starts offering solutions. When she tells him about a problem she is having with a co-worker, he has a ready answer. When she shares a concern she has about her relationship with her supervisor, he tells her she worries too much. When she relates a problem one of the children is having with a classmate, he dismisses it as if it were nothing. "Don't get yourself all worked up," he says. "Let them work it out."

Finally she gives up in exasperation and heads for the kitchen to begin dinner. Sensing her obvious frustration he shouts after her, "Joyce, what are you upset about?" Slamming a cupboard door, she says, "Why can't you just listen to me?"

What we have here is a classic male/female misunderstanding. As a general rule, when a man shares a problem, he is looking for a solution. On the other hand, when a woman talks about her concerns, she is simply looking for understanding. When he puts on his Mr. Fix-It hat and begins solving her problems, she feels that he is invalidating her feelings, which only leaves her more frustrated. When she continues to be upset after he has offered his solutions, it becomes increasingly difficult for him to listen because he feels useless, never realizing that all she wants is his empathy.

The real problem here is timing. A woman greatly appreciates her husband's problem-solving ability as long as he doesn't try to fix things when she's upset. At that time his advice is about as welcome as "...one who takes away a garment on a cold day...."[1] As Dr. John Gray points out in *Men Are From Mars, Women Are From Venus*, "Men need to remember that women talk about problems to get close and not necessarily to get solutions."[2]

ACTION STEPS:

▼ THE NEXT TIME YOUR WIFE BEGINS TO SHARE HER PROBLEMS, BITE YOUR TONGUE. INSTEAD OF OFFERING ADVICE, GIVE HER YOUR SHOULDER TO CRY ON. IN TIME SHE WILL SOLVE HER OWN PROBLEMS, AND SHE WILL THINK YOU ARE THE MOST UNDERSTANDING MAN IN ALL THE WORLD.

▼ MAKE IT A POINT TO READ *MEN ARE FROM MARS, WOMEN ARE FROM VENUS* (HARPERCOLLINS) BY JOHN GRAY, PH.D., AND DISCUSS IT WITH YOUR WIFE.

THOUGHT FOR THE DAY:

"How had I missed this? She just needed me to go over and hold her. Another woman would have instinctively known what Bonnie needed. But as a man, I didn't know that touching, holding, and listening were so important to her. By recognizing these differences I began to learn a new way of relating to my wife."[3]

John Gray, Ph.D.

SCRIPTURE FOR THE DAY:
Like one who takes away a garment on a cold day, or like vinegar poured on soda, is one who sings songs to a heavy heart.
PROVERBS 25:20

✟

PRAYER:

LORD, I LIKE TO BE THE HERO, RIDING IN ON MY WHITE HORSE AND SOLVING ALL THE PROBLEMS. I'VE NEVER STOPPED TO REALIZE THAT WHEN I RESCUE MY WIFE, I MAKE HER FEEL LIKE A HELPLESS VICTIM. TEACH ME TO BE MORE SENSITIVE TO HER FEELINGS AND LESS CONCERNED ABOUT MY OWN. IN THE NAME OF JESUS I PRAY. AMEN.

---

[1] Proverbs 25:20.
[2] John Gray, Ph.D., *Men Are From Mars, Women Are From Venus* (New York: HarperCollins Publishers, Inc., 1992), p. 21.
[3] Ibid., p. 2.

CHAPTER 54

A NIGHT TO REMEMBER

One of the things I admired most about the congregation I served in Tulsa, Oklahoma, was their compassion, their willingness to give of themselves, and their resources to help others who were less fortunate. For instance, one Christmas I received a call from a couple in the church who wanted to know if I knew of a needy family, someone with whom they could share Christmas.

"What," I asked, "do you have in mind?"

"Well," he said, "I thought that you might be aware of a special situation, a family who won't have much of a Christmas unless they get some help. What we would like to do is buy some groceries, and some presents for the children. And if it's all right, we would like to take it to them. Not so we can appear to be great philanthropists, but to make it somehow more personal. We don't just want to give groceries and things. We want to give something of ourselves as well."

I knew just the family, a desperate situation. A few weeks earlier the mother had called and shared her painful story.

She was divorced, trying to rear two children alone, and unemployed. To make matters worse, her youngest son had leukemia. In addition to the obvious financial difficulties and the trauma of her son's illness, she was pregnant. The father was a married man, a leader in the church where she had attended. She never had any intention of becoming involved with him. It just happened.

While he was providing pastoral care for her, during a critical time in her son's illness, an emotional bond had been formed between them. In a moment of weakness, this bond resulted in a sexual encounter that was completely unpremeditated.

Recognizing that their actions were sinful and potentially destructive, they immediately terminated the relationship, but the damage had already been done. As soon as she realized that she was pregnant, she decided to leave the church rather than risk damaging the father's family or jeopardizing his position in the church. Now she was alone, without family or friends, or a support system of any kind.

Our office contacted her by telephone, and after getting her permission, we made the necessary arrangements. That was the last I heard about it until a few days after Christmas when that generous couple dropped by the office to give me a report. It was, according to them, the highlight of their Christmas season. And no wonder, for there is something about an unselfish act that is its own reward. You can't give love away without getting it back, in good measure, pressed down, and running over.

That couple and their three children had gone out there to make Christmas for that desperate mother and her two small sons. Instead, they discovered that God had made a Christmas for them. Years from now, when their own children have long since forgotten the presents they received, they will undoubtedly recall the magic of making Christmas for someone less fortunate than themselves.

Only God knows what their act of kindness meant to that destitute family. I have to believe that their presence meant more than the presents they brought. Because as bad as that little family needed groceries, as poverty-stricken as they were, as bleak as their Christmas might have been, what they needed more than anything else was the warmth and the reality of genuine fellowship.

ACTION STEPS:

▼ REMEMBER A TIME WHEN YOU WERE ON THE RECEIVING END OF A GENUINELY COMPASSIONATE ACT. HOW DID IT MAKE YOU FEEL?

▼ REMEMBER A TIME WHEN YOU EXPRESSED GENUINE COMPASSION TO ANOTHER PERSON. HOW DID IT MAKE YOU FEEL?

▼ MAKE A CONSCIOUS EFFORT TO BE AWARE OF OPPORTUNITIES WHERE YOU AND YOUR FAMILY CAN EXPRESS GODLY COMPASSION.

THOUGHT FOR THE DAY:

"Generosity is not merely a trait which pleases God. It is a practice which releases us from bondage to the ego, and also to things.... There is no place where the lives of saintly people bear a clearer witness. They have all undertaken the disciplines of generosity."[1]

Albert E. Day

SCRIPTURE FOR THE DAY:

Love must be sincere. Hate what is evil; cling to what is good.
Be devoted to one another in brotherly love. Honor one another
above yourselves. Never be lacking in zeal, but keep your spiritual fervor,
serving the Lord. Be joyful in hope, patient in affliction, faithful in
prayer. Share with God's people who are in need. Practice hospitality.

ROMANS 12:9-13

PRAYER:

LORD JESUS, YOU HAVE GIVEN ME SO MUCH, MORE THAN
I COULD EVER DESERVE. GRANT ME ONE THING MORE—
A GENEROUS SPIRIT. IN YOUR HOLY NAME I PRAY.

---

[1] Albert E. Day, *Discipline and Discovery* quoted in *Disciplines for the Inner Life* by Bob Benson and Michael W. Benson (Waco: Word Book Publishers, 1985), pp. 252, 253.

CHAPTER 55

THE MUD OR THE STARS

As my ten-year-old daughter hurried toward the car I could tell something was wrong, and when she slid onto the front seat beside me she burst into tears. Looking at her sitting there with tears running down her cheeks, I thought my heart would break. I wanted to take her in my arms and shield her from the world. I wanted to protect her from all the pain and cruelty that we human beings heap on each other, but I knew I couldn't. Instead, I held her hand and listened as she poured out her anger and humiliation.

When she finally exhausted her tearful rage, I suggested that we go somewhere and have a hamburger. She agreed, and in a matter of minutes, we were seated in a corner booth munching on some fries. While we ate, I told her a story: During the Second World War a young lady named Thelma Thompson and her soldier husband were stationed at an Army training camp near the Mojave Desert in California. According to Thelma she went to live there to be near her husband.

She says, "I hated the place. I loathed it. I had never before been so miserable. My husband was ordered out on maneuvers in the Mojave Desert, and I was left in a tiny shack, alone. The heat was unbearable—125 degrees in the shade of a cactus. Not a soul to talk to but Mexicans and Indians, and they couldn't speak English. The wind blew incessantly, and all the food I ate, and the very air I breathed, was filled with sand, sand, sand!

"I was so utterly wretched, so sorry for myself, that I wrote to my parents. I told them I was giving up and coming home. I said I couldn't stand it one minute longer. I would rather be in jail! My father answered my letter with just two lines—two lines that will always sing in my memory—two lines that completely altered my life:

'Two men looked out from prison bars,

One saw the mud, the other saw the stars.'

"I read those two lines over and over. I was ashamed of myself. I made up my mind I would look for the stars. I made friends with the natives, and their reaction amazed me. When I showed interest in their weaving and pottery, they gave me presents of their favorite pieces, which they had refused to show to the tourists. I studied the fascinating forms of the cactus and the yuccas and the Joshua trees. I learned about prairie dogs, watched for the desert sunsets, and hunted for seashells that had been left there millions of years ago when the sands of the desert had been an ocean floor.

"What brought about this astonishing change in me? The Mojave Desert hadn't changed. The Indians hadn't changed. But I had. I had changed my attitude of mind. And by doing so, I transformed a wretched experience into the most exciting adventure of my life. I was stimulated and excited by this new world that I had discovered. I was so excited I wrote a book about it—a novel that was published under the title *Bright Ramparts*. I had looked out of my self-created prison and found the stars."[1]

"Leah," I said, reaching for her hands, "you won't always have the power to change the circumstances in which you find yourself, but you always have the power to choose your attitude. So what's it going to be, girl, are you going to look at the mud or the stars?"

From that day forward those two lines became a motto in our family. Whenever some childhood disappointment or adolescent difficulty tempted Leah to depression I simply asked, "What are you looking at sweetheart, the mud or the stars?" The choice wasn't always easy, but inevitably her chin would come up and with a look of fierce determination she would say, "I choose to look at the stars!"

One Sunday evening, when Leah was maybe thirteen or fourteen, I was complaining to Brenda as we drove toward the church. The particulars of that conversation have long since been forgotten, but I do recall that I was putting on quite a show. Suddenly, from the backseat, I heard this adolescent voice:

"'Two men looked out from prison bars,

One saw the mud, the other saw the stars.'

What are you going to be Dad, a star gazer or a mud sucker?"

Now, I don't mind telling you that, in spite of being soundly rebuked, that was an unforgettable moment for me. Indeed, it would have been for any father. For a man never knows a prouder moment than when he hears the spiritual values he has endeavored to impress upon his children repeated back to him. In that moment I understood a little more of what Solomon meant when he wrote: "Pleasant words are a honeycomb, sweet to the soul and healing to the bones."[2]

ACTION STEPS:

▼ TAKE A FEW MINUTES AND REMINISCE. CAN YOU RECALL A TIME WHEN ONE OF YOUR PARENTS SPOKE HEALING, EVEN LIFE-CHANGING WORDS, TO YOU? IF YOUR PARENTS ARE STILL LIVING, WHY NOT WRITE THEM A NOTE AND THANK THEM.

▼ AS A HUSBAND AND A FATHER, YOUR WORDS HAVE TREMENDOUS POWER FOR YOUR WIFE AND CHILDREN. DETERMINE RIGHT NOW THAT YOU WILL SPEAK WORDS OF LIFE AND NOT DEATH, THAT YOU WILL AFFIRM AND ENCOURAGE YOUR FAMILY AT EVERY OPPORTUNITY.

▼ MEMORIZE PSALM 141:3, "SET A GUARD OVER MY MOUTH, O LORD; KEEP WATCH OVER THE DOOR OF MY LIPS." MAKE THAT YOUR DAILY PRAYER.

THOUGHT FOR THE DAY:

"Benjamin West, a British artist, tells how he first became aware of his artistic skills. One day his mother went out, leaving him in charge of his little sister Sally. In his mother's absence, he discovered some bottles of colored ink and to amuse her, he began to paint Sally's portrait. In doing so, he made quite a mess of things...spilled numerous ink splotches here and there. When his mother returned, she saw the mess, but said nothing about it. She deliberately looked beyond all that as she picked up the piece of paper. Smiling, she exclaimed, 'Why, it's Sally!' She then stooped and kissed her son.

From that time on, Benjamin West would say, 'My mother's kiss made me a painter.'"[3]

William Barclay

SCRIPTURE FOR THE DAY:

When Isaac caught the smell of his clothes, he blessed him and said,
"Ah, the smell of my son
is like the smell of a field
that the LORD has blessed.
May God give you of heaven's dew
and of earth's richness—
an abundance of grain and new wine.
May nations serve you
and peoples bow down to you.
Be lord over your brothers,
and may the sons of your mother
bow down to you.
May those who curse you be cursed
and those who bless you be blessed."

GENESIS 27:27-29

PRAYER:

LORD, I HAVE TO CONFESS THAT MORE OFTEN THAN NOT I HAVE EYES ONLY FOR THE MESS. IN SORROW, I HAVE TO WONDER HOW MANY NASCENT DREAMS I HAVE CRUSHED WITH A CARELESS WORD. FORGIVE ME, LORD, AND SET A GUARD OVER MY MOUTH AND A WATCH OVER THE DOOR OF MY LIPS. IN THE NAME OF JESUS I PRAY. AMEN.

---

[1]   C. Roy Angell, *Baskets of Silver* (Nashville, TN: Broadman Press, 1955) pp. 102-104.
[2]   Proverbs 16:24.
[3]   Taken from *The Daily Study Bible*, "The Letters to the Galatians and Ephesians" by William Barclay (Edinburgh, Scotland: The Saint Andrew Press, 1962), p. 211.

CHAPTER 56

HOLY HUGS

As I stepped out of the car, a gust of wind caused the cold to pierce me like a knife. Involuntarily, I tugged up the collar of my overcoat and tried to burrow into its warmth. *Thank God I've got a home,* I thought. *Life on the streets would be deadly in this weather.*

"You's gots some wools, man?"

The voice was raspy, harsh sounding, and when I turned to see who had spoken, he began pleading. "I's needs some wools bad. I's freezen in dis col."

He stood there shivering as I looked him up and down. I guessed him to be about forty, but he looked older. His lips were cracked from the cold, and his skin was chapped and raw. The jacket he was wearing had a broken zipper and was badly worn, especially at the elbows where the lining was showing through. Underneath he wore something resembling a cardigan sweater over a faded flannel shirt.

Standing there with the north wind tugging at my wool coat, my mind flashed back to the series of events that had brought me to this moment. For days God had been dealing with me about the plight of the homeless. It seemed that every time I turned on the television there was another special about some family living under a bridge or in their car. As Christmas drew near, and an unexpected cold spell plunged temperatures near zero degrees, I felt more and more compelled to do something, but what.

Each time I prayed God seemed to remind me of a double-breasted, navy blue overcoat hanging in my closet. It was nearly ten years old but hardly looked worn. For warmth and durability, it was the best coat I had ever owned. A couple of years earlier I had replaced it with a newer style, but I couldn't bear to part with it, so I kept it hanging in the downstairs coat closet. Now it was a sore point between the Lord and me. I sensed He wanted me to give it to some homeless person, but I couldn't bring myself to part with it.

During my devotional time that morning, God spoke to me so clearly that I knew I could resist no longer. After telling my secretary that I was leaving, I drove home to collect the coat and a matching wool scarf. When Brenda asked me how I would know who to give it to, I answered, "God will show me; and if He doesn't, I will just give it to Mother Tucker's rescue mission."

That's where I was now—in front of Mother Tucker's—being harassed by this...this homeless wino. In disgust, I turned my back on him and opened the rear door of my car. When he saw me take the coat out of the car, his eyes lit up with desire. "I's needs some wools, man..." he began as I ignored him and started walking toward the front door of the mission. He followed me, pleading, and as I started to open the door, it hit me. He was the answer to my prayer, the man to whom God wanted me to give my coat.

I turned so swiftly that I almost bumped into him. Thrusting the coat at him I said, "Here, try this on."

In an instant he had the coat on and buttoned up. It fit perfectly, as I knew it would. Stepping closer, I put the matching wool scarf around his neck and tucked it inside the front of his coat. Before I could step back, he wrapped his arms around me and pulled me to his chest in a bear hug. He smelled like booze and body odor and damp clothes, but I didn't mind. His was the holiest hug I've ever received. In that moment it was as if God Himself were hugging me.

ACTION STEPS:

▼ IN PRAYER, ASK GOD TO GIVE YOU A COMPASSIONATE HEART FOR ALL OF THOSE LESS FORTUNATE THAN YOURSELF.

▼ IS THERE ANYONE IN YOUR IMMEDIATE CIRCLE OF FRIENDS AND ASSOCI-ATES WHO IS IN NEED? A SINGLE PARENT PERHAPS WHO CANNOT AFFORD TO SEND HER SON TO CHURCH CAMP? A NEWLYWED COUPLE WHO NEEDS SOME HELP REPAIRING THEIR CAR? IF YOU CAN'T THINK OF ANYONE, ASK YOUR PASTOR. HE IS PROBABLY AWARE OF SOME DESPER-ATE NEED WITHIN THE CHURCH FAMILY.

▼ IN PRAYER, ASK GOD WHAT HE WOULD HAVE YOU TO DO TO MEET THESE NEEDS. BE SENSITIVE TO THE THOUGHTS AND IMPRESSIONS THAT COME TO YOU AS YOU WAIT QUIETLY BEFORE HIM. THAT'S USUALLY HOW HE SPEAKS TO US. NOW GO AND DO AS HE DIRECTS YOU.

THOUGHT FOR THE DAY:

"Going to town one day to sell some small articles, Abba Agathon met a cripple on the roadside, paralyzed in his legs, who asked him where he was going. Abba Agathon replied, 'To town, to sell some things.' The other said, 'Do me the favor of carrying me there.' So he carried him to the town. The cripple said to him, 'Put me down where you sell your wares.' He did so. When he had sold an article, the cripple asked, 'What did you sell it for?' and he told him the price. The other said, 'Buy me a cake,' and he bought it. When Abba Agathon had sold all his wares, wanted to go, he said to him, 'Are you going back?' and he replied, 'Yes.' Then he said, 'Do me the favor of carrying me back to the place where you found me.' Once more picking him up, he carried him back to that place. Then the cripple said, 'Agathon, you are filled with divine blessings, in heaven and on earth.' Raising his eyes, Agathon saw no man; it was an angel of the Lord, come to try him."[1]

The Desert Christian

SCRIPTURE FOR THE DAY:

"One man gives freely, yet gains even more; another withholds unduly, but comes to poverty. A generous man will prosper; he who refreshes others will himself be refreshed."

PROVERBS 11:24-25

PRAYER:

LORD, THANK YOU FOR LETTING ME KNOW THE JOY OF SHARING WITH THOSE LESS FORTUNATE THAN I. FORGIVE ME FOR THE TIMES I AM BLIND OR INSENSITIVE TO THEIR NEEDS. DON'T GIVE UP ON ME. SURELY ONE DAY I WILL BE THE MAN YOU HAVE CALLED ME TO BE. IN THE NAME OF JESUS I PRAY. AMEN.

---

[1] *The Desert Christian*, translated by Benedicta Ward, quoted in *Disciplines for the Inner Life* by Bob Benson and Michael W. Benson, (Waco: Word Books Publisher, 1985), pp. 251, 252.

A True Man of Valor

It is late August and though fall is only days away, the stubborn summer heat blankets the high plains of northeastern Colorado. The only relief comes early each morning, but by midday the heat has returned and the cool of autumn seems hardly more than a distant hope. I should remember the August heat, but I don't. Time has erased all but the fondest memories of my childhood, and it has been more than twenty years since I have visited the place of my birth in late summer.

It is something of a disappointment to discover that the Sterling I return to in no way resembles the hometown I remember. The house on Villa Vista, which loomed so large in my memory, is modest—small if the truth be known—and my Grandma Miller's old house, where I knew such happiness as a boy, is hardly more than a shack. Still, not even their dusty tiredness can dim the joy of my boyhood memories. In those bygone days, love and laughter made every day seem like Saturday.

With a start I realize that Uncle Ernie's funeral—my reason for being here—is scheduled to begin shortly. Allowing myself one last look around, I return to the car and drive quickly to the church.

As I sit on the platform watching the congregation file in, a host of memories wash over me. It was here, in this very church, that as a child of nine I was baptized in water and where two years later I would experience the infilling of the Holy Spirit. It was here that I first sang the great hymns of the faith and where I formulated my earliest understanding of God.

With an effort, I turn my attention to the present. The faces before me are familiar but different. The energetic adults of my childhood are gone and in their places sit old people who have come today to mourn the passing of a dear friend, and on another level, to contemplate their own mortality. How swiftly time flies, I think, how soon we grow old.

I focus my gaze on the second pew where the family sits. My father is there, with Mother at his side, looking more vulnerable than I remember. Without question the years have taken their toll. His thinning hair is completely gray now, nearly white really, as is his beard. Today there is pain in his face and his shoulders are bowed with weariness and grief. Gone is my seemingly indestructible father, and in his place sits this frail stranger, looking somehow small and uncertain before the relentless march of time.

My Aunt Elsie sits beside him, wrinkled now and stoop-shouldered from osteoporosis. Even my seemingly ageless Uncle Denny is finally succumbing to the inevitable erosion of the years. He has resisted longer than most; but now his step, too, is slowed, his strength waning.

Every silver hair, each and every wrinkle, the slowed steps, the quiet reminiscing all testify to mankind's mortality and to mine. Unconsciously I find myself reciting a poem from my childhood, etched indelibly on my memory by at least a half a hundred sermons that I heard, as a child, sitting in this very sanctuary.

"Only one life, t'will soon be passed,

Only what's done for Jesus will last."

With the casket, prominently displayed directly in front of the pulpit, I cannot help but ponder the meaning of life. When our days on earth are done, when we look back on how we have lived our lives, what will be important to us then?

Organ music announces the start of the service, and my thoughts turn once again to Uncle Ernie and the life he lived. He was not a great man as the world counts greatness. He never served as the pastor of a large church, he never wrote a book, nor did he make a name for himself. He was, however, a man of valor—a throwback to an earlier age when the measure of a man was determined by the quality of his character rather than the power of his personality. In truth, he was one of those men who "wore well"—that is, the longer you knew him the more you appreciated him.

Most of his adult life was spent serving small country churches. Though his congregations loved him dearly, they simply did not have the means to support a pastor. Being energetic and something of an entrepreneur, he managed to make ends meet. For a while he operated a service station when that meant not only pumping gas and washing windshields, but also running a grease rack and fixing flats.

In the mid-sixties he spent a couple of summers doing custom swathing, while serving a small church in Haxtun, Colorado. He even tried his hand at breeding Appaloosa horses for a short time, but his mainstay was painting houses. Don't misunderstand me. His first love was the ministry, no one who knew him could doubt that, everything else was just "tent making," just a way to provide for his family.

If you don't look beneath the surface, Uncle Ernie's life appears rather insignificant, but on a deeper level it has eternal value. Only God knows how many men and women received Jesus Christ as their

Savior as a result of his witness, and who can measure the value of a single soul?

Even in death his ministry lives on. He had a profound influence on my brother Don and his decision to become a missionary. Another nephew, Orville Stewart, is a pastor, and Uncle Ernie's ministry lives on in his work also. Of course, anything I do and whatever influence I have are his as well. He gave me my start in the ministry and invited me to preach in every church where he served as pastor. He was a special friend and my first spiritual mentor.

When I was just a boy preacher of sixteen, I telephoned him to ask if I could preach a revival meeting in his church. Only now, these many years later, do I realize how presumptuous that was. Nonetheless, he opened his pulpit to me.

Before the first service, he offered to critique my sermons. Of course I agreed, not because I felt a need for his expertise, but simply because I knew of no way to tell him that it wouldn't be necessary, without appearing immodest.

My first sermon was more legalism than gospel, but what I lacked in theology I more than made up for with my feverish enthusiasm. With a zeal that now seems frightening, I preached about the Great White Throne Judgment. In truth, I dangled those poor saints over hell on a rotting stick. When I finally finished, I was quite pleased with myself.

Uncle Ernie didn't seem very eager to critique my sermon and who could blame him? I mean, how do you tell your sixteen-year-old nephew that he is one of the finest preachers you have ever heard, without exposing him to the deadliest of all ministerial temptations—pride? Imagine my chagrin when we finally entered his study, late the next day, and he proceeded to dismantle my sermon with surgical skill.

When he finally finished, I was absolutely devastated. Although it was one of the most painful experiences of my life, I can truthfully say it was also one of the most helpful. The foundations for all that I am today, as a preacher and as a minister, were laid that afternoon. Needless to say, I will be forever grateful that Uncle Ernie cared enough to risk offending me in order to get me started right.

When old age and failing health made it impossible for him to continue in full-time ministry, he retired to Sterling, Colorado, to be near his wife's family. Although he was officially retired, he remained active in the local Assembly. Not only did he minister to senior adults, but as was in keeping with the servant's heart that had characterized his entire ministry, he also provided custodial services for the church.

Maybe the most important ministry he had was to his pastor, a man half his age. Uncle Ernie loved him and respected him, as only a man who had nearly fifty years in the ministry could. He prayed for him daily and supported him in every way. He provided wise counsel when it was sought, but mostly he was a ready listener. His was a shoulder to lean on.

Thinking about him now I can only conclude that what set Uncle Ernie apart was his character. Not once in nearly fifty years of ministry did anyone have an occasion to question his personal integrity. When some poor business decisions pushed him to the point of financial ruin, he temporarily left the ministry in order to repay his creditors rather than file bankruptcy and bring a reproach on the church.

How different he was from those ministers for whom image is everything. They worry about appearances—wearing the right clothes, driving the right car, knowing the right people, even being the pastor of the right church. Uncle Ernie, on the other hand, concerned himself with matters of personal integrity. Congruity was important to him. What he appeared to be and what he truly was had to be one and the same. To his way of thinking substance was more important than show.

Although character of this nature is rare, it is not complicated. You simply choose the needs of others over your own. You live modestly, love your neighbor as yourself, turn the other cheek, forgive others as Christ has forgiven you, keep your word, pay your debts on time, and honor your commitments. You provide for your family, honor your marriage vows, love your spouse, train your children in the nurture and admonition of the Lord, and honor the Lord in all you do and say.

This is what the apostle Paul was talking about when he instructed Timothy to, "Be diligent in these matters; give yourself wholly to them, so that everyone may see your progress. Watch your life and doctrine closely. Persevere in them, because if you do, you will save both yourself and your hearers."[1]

The pastor is nearing the end of his sermon and my thoughts return to the present. Around me the congregation dabs at damp eyes. For a moment they are gone from this small sanctuary, fragrant on this hot August afternoon with the scent of funeral sprays. They are gone to a time somewhere in the past. To a moment when Uncle Ernie touched and enriched their lives even as he did my own. Like me, they are challenged by his selflessness, by the way he gave so freely of himself to the Lord he loved more than life, and to others.

Truly he was a man of valor!

---

[1] 1 Timothy 4:15-16.

ABOUT THE AUTHOR

Richard Exley is an intense person who cares deeply for people. This compassion is reflected in all his endeavors. He is a man with a rich diversity of experience—pastor, author, radio host, conference and retreat speaker. After serving churches in Colorado,  Texas, and Oklahoma for twenty-six years, he now devotes his time fully to writing and speaking.

When he is not speaking at retreats and conferences across the country, Richard and his wife, Brenda Starr, spend their time in a secluded cabin overlooking picturesque Beaver Lake. Richard enjoys quiet talks with old friends, kerosene lamps, good books, a warm fire when it is cold, and a good cup of coffee anytime. He's an avid Denver Broncos fan, an aspiring bass fisherman, and an amateur photographer.

For additional information on seminars, scheduling speaking engagements, or to write the author, please address your correspondence to:

Richard Exley
P. O. Box 54744
Tulsa, Oklahoma 74155

Or call: 918-459-5434

or visit: www.richardexleyministry.org

Additional copies of this book and other titles by Richard Exley
are available from your local bookstore.

If this book has touched your life we would love to hear from you.

Please write us at:

White Stone Books
P. O. Box 2835
Lakeland, Florida 33806

"...To him who overcomes I will give some of the hidden manna to eat.
And I will give him a white stone, and on the stone a new name
written which no one knows except him who receives it."

REVELATION 2:17 NKJV

Visit our website at:
www.whitestonebooks.com

WHITE STONE BOOKS
LAKELAND, FLORIDA